TW-121

The Proper Care of
Dwarf Rabbits

Michael Mettler

Photo credits: Toni Angermayer, Bruce Crook, Isabelle Français, Michael Gilroy, H. Hanson, Burkhard Kahl, Louise Van der Meid, Michael Mettler, Ingeborg Polaschek, Reinhard-Tierfoto, D. Robinson, Vince Serbin, Sally Anne Thompson, Vitakraft (Willy Winkler), and XENIEL-Dia (Ernst Müller).

Drawings: V.D. Kolganov, A.N. Sitchar, F.E. Terletsky, F. Voitov, and V.V. Zotov.

The Proper Care of
Dwarf Rabbits

Michael Mettler

translated by
U. Erich Friese

Because of the growing international appeal of the rabbit hobby as a whole, this book includes illustrations of rabbits not only from the USA and the UK but also from Germany and Russia. (The reader may recognize particular rabbit breeds but may be unfamiliar with their nomenclature, as this, of course, varies from country to country.)

Distributed in the UNITED STATES by T.F.H. Publications, Inc., One T.F.H. Plaza, Neptune City, NJ 07753; in CANADA to the Pet Trade by H & L Pet Supplies Inc., 27 Kingston Crescent, Kitchener, Ontario N2B 2T6; Rolf C. Hagen Ltd., 3225 Sartelon Street, Montreal 382 Quebec; in CANADA to the Book Trade by Macmillan of Canada (A Division of Canada Publishing Corporation), 164 Commander Boulevard, Agincourt, Ontario M1S 3C7; in ENGLAND by T.F.H. Publications, PO Box 15, Waterlooville PO7 6BQ; in AUSTRALIA AND THE SOUTH PACIFIC by T.F.H. (Australia) Pty. Ltd., Box 149, Brookvale 2100 N.S.W., Australia; in NEW ZEALAND by Ross Haines & Son, Ltd., 82 D Elizabeth Knox Place, Panmure, Auckland, New Zealand; in the PHILIPPINES by Bio-Research, 5 Lippay Street, San Lorenzo Village, Makati, Rizal; in SOUTH AFRICA by Multipet Pty. Ltd., P.O. Box 35347, Northway, 4065, South Africa. Published by T.F.H. Publications, Inc. Manufactured in the United States of America by T.F.H. Publications, Inc.

Contents

For many years, rabbits were grouped in the order Rodentia, a large mammalian group commonly called rodents. Today, they (along with hares and pikas) are classed in the order Lagomorpha.

Origin and History

You may be surprised to read that rabbits are not rodents, and consequently they are not related to two other small traditional household pets: hamsters and guinea pigs. For a long time, hares and rabbits had been considered as rodents because of their gnawing teeth. Yet, anatomists noticed early on that there are certain differences, especially in the skeletal structure of the jaw. The most important characteristic of hares—the correct zoological terminology for these animals—is a small pair of teeth located directly behind the large incisors; these are small pin-like incisors (without a cutting edge) and are absent in true rodents. Because of this anatomical peculiarity, hares and rabbits were once referred to as double-toothed animals (Duplicidentata) and were placed into a different systematic group. It was not until early in the twentieth

Although the dwarf rabbit and guinea pig are similar in appearance, they are not related at all.

century that hares and rabbits were 'elevated' into their own zoological order, Lagomorpha.

The development of specialized 'gnawing' dentition has occurred among mammals repeatedly but always independently of any phylogenetic relationship. For instance, chisel-like incisors are also found in marsupials such as wombats, as well as in the strange-looking Madagascan lemur, the aye-aye. Consequently, one speaks of parallel development because of similar feeding behavior. Zoologists describe this phenomenon as convergent evolution. According to current scientific opinion, hares and rabbits are not even distantly related to rodents; for instance,

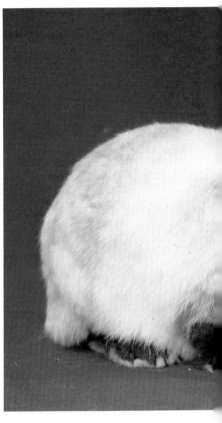

A seal point Holland Lop. These diminutive rabbits are the smallest of the Lop breeds.

they do not share the same ancestors. Anatomical details support closer relationships to hoofed animals, especially to the Artiodactyla (even-toed ungulates), which include pigs, camels, and deer. At some stage it had also been assumed that hares and rabbits were phylogenetically close to the extinct ancestral carnivore animals. These, in turn, are supposed to be related to the ancestral hoofed animals. The true rodents, however, are now considered to be close to primates—the great apes, as well as man.

The Lagomorpha are divided into two families. First, there is the family Ochotonidae, the so-called pikas, which are small, mostly burrowing animals. There are about 15 species of these rabbit-like animals; all are of rather uniform external appearance. There is a superficial resemblance to hamsters and guinea pigs, but they are indeed true 'rabbits.' Pikas live in the mountain regions of Asia and North America. They communicate with each other by means of a sharp or shrill whistle. Sometimes they are also called whistling hares.

The largest number of

There are over 40 breeds of rabbit recognized throughout the world.

hare-like animals belongs to the family Leporidae. It contains about 45 species, which were originally distributed over all the continents, except Australia. We know, of course, that today even the smallest continent has large populations of the European wild rabbit (introduced to Australia by the early settlers). The Leporidae include all species that we now call hares and rabbits.

HARE OR RABBIT?

Rabbits and hares are closely related animals and share a basically similar appearance. However, there are notable differences, both physical and behavioral, and these can be better appreciated by taking a look at two hare-like animals commonly found in Central Europe.

Firstly, there is the common European hare *(Lepus europaeus)*, also known as the field hare. With an impressive head-to-rump length of 20 to 30 in. (50 to 76 cm), it can reach the size of a domesticated tom cat. Its weight can be as much as 15.3 lbs. (6.5 kg). Some exceptional specimens have weighed in at 17.6 lbs. (8 kg). Legs and ears are very long, and the latter have conspicuous black tips. The abdomen is pure white, and the golden-

Like the other breeds of rabbit shown here, Netherland Dwarfs (bottom left) come in a variety of colors and patterns.

brown back is sprinkled with a salt-and-pepper pattern (the so-called agouti coloration). The iris is distinctly lighter than the pupil, so that field hares have a somewhat 'staring' look.

On the other hand, the European wild rabbit (*Oryctolagus cuniculus*) reaches a length of only 15.2 to 20 in. (38 to 50 cm) and a weight of 1.98 to 4.4 lbs. (.9 to 2 kg, sometimes to 3 kg). Its legs and ears are much shorter, and the latter are lacking black tips. The abdominal region is grayish white, and the back is gray to grayish

A pair of Netherland Dwarf rabbits: white and
Himalayan marked.

brown with a reddish triangular-shaped patch on the back of the neck. Because of a dark iris, the wild rabbit has a notably wide-eyed look.

There are even more conspicuous behavioral differences among the

The wild rabbit is the ancestor of all domesticated rabbit breeds. (Note how its coloration camouflages the animal against the background.)

Even though it may pose as Duerer's "Hare," a dwarf hare is not a hare but a rabbit.

species. The field hare lives in open fields and avoids dense forests. It does not burrow but stays in shallow dug-out pits. When danger approaches, the animal presses its body close to the ground or to the bottom of its pit and relies principally on its superb camouflage coloration. Only when approached too closely will the animal jump up and race off at great speed.

You can bring a lot of joy to your pet with a handful of fresh grass or dandelions. Just make sure the greens are collected from an uncontaminated area.

The Belgian Hare, in spite of its name, is, in fact, a rabbit.

Wild rabbits, on the other hand, prefer ground with lots of cover, e.g., bushland, inner and outer forests, as well as the rolling hills of a country side. They dig burrows with several entrances, where they rest, sleep, and retreat in case of danger. Rabbits are sprinters, while hares can maintain high speeds up to 42 mi. (70 km) per hour!

Differences in breeding behavior are also conspicuous. Field hares have a gestation period of 42 to 43 days

Body conformation in rabbits can vary from lithe and slender to thickset and stocky.

litters (up to 9, rarely 14) are produced. The young are born in underground nesting burrows, which the female pads with some of her own abdominal fur. At birth, these young rabbits are naked, blind, and totally helpless (altricial young).

So, when you go for a walk and come across a rather large 'longear' sitting alone in the middle of a field or paddock, it is probably a field hare. The small animals often seen dashing about in packs (even alongside busy roads) and that burrow

and then produce two or three fully developed young. They are already completely covered with fur, the eyes are open, and they are capable of running (precocial young). The female does not build a nest for the young; instead they stay in shallow pits just like adults.

The gestation period for rabbits is shorter (28 to 31 days), and larger

Opposite: Belgian Hare. Note the sleekness of its fur.

under fences and annoy garden owners by nibbling on their precious flowers, are invariably wild rabbits. By the way, both species are capable of performing spectacular cross-directional leaps when in full flight.

From these differences we can clearly see that hare and rabbit are about as related as dog and fox. All breeds of domesticated rabbit have the wild rabbit as their ancestor.

MORPHOLOGY AND SENSORY PERCEPTION

We have already discussed a few morphological peculiarities of hares and rabbits. Now let us look at a few more details. Long ears are the most conspicuous feature in

Belgian Hare. At one time, it was thought that these rabbits could be bred to true wild hares, but this is not true.

all rabbit-like animals. These ears not only serve as auditory receptors but also serve as effective temperature regulators. The highly vascularized ears (equipped with many tiny blood vessels) are excellent in giving off excess body heat. If a rabbit's body temperature is elevated, the ears feel distinctly warm to the touch. If a rabbit is very cold, it will press its ears closely against its body and 'compact' itself in order to conserve body heat. Consequently, it may not necessarily have been a joke when a British newspaper reported a few years ago that a gardener was heating his greenhouse with excess body heat given off by rabbits' ears!

A rabbit's eyes are large and round. They are well adapted to help the animal get around during dusk and dawn periods. Consequently, you do not have to leave the lights clearly see how the black pupil stands out against the light blue iris. This gives the animal an almost piercing look.

A rabbit has a so-called panoramic view of things

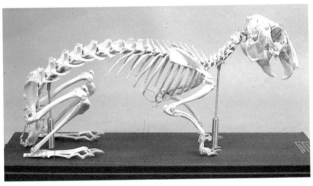

Skeletal specimen of the domestic rabbit *Oryctolagus cuniculus.*

on at night when you want to go to bed but your pet rabbit is still feeding! The rabbit's eye does not consist of a very large pupil, as you will notice once you look into the eyes of a blue-eyed rabbit. Here you can

Opposite: Cute and cuddly... Who can resist the charms of a dwarf rabbit?

Do not let your rabbit have access to dogbane, darnel grass, and veratrum (left to right), all of which are poisonous.

Some hobbyists offer burdock (left) as a treat food. Stinging nettle (right) should be avoided because it can act as an irritant.

around it due to the lateral position of the eyes on the head. In fact, it can even see what is going on behind its back, without having to turn its rabbit starts to feed. The nose has another characteristic as well: when a rabbit is awake, its nose is virtually in continuous motion in

head. Not only are hearing (because of the large ears) and sight well developed in rabbits, but so is their sense of smell. All food is always carefully sniffed before a

Above: A Dutch male.

Opposite: Female (top) and male (bottom) white Giants.

order to monitor the odors in the surrounding area. These nostril movements are due to the fact that the nostrils are covered by a skin fold that is retracted continuously. This is sometimes referred to as 'nostril batting' or 'blinking.'

The upper lip is split, and so it forms essentially two (upper) lips. This morphological feature is the so-called 'hare lip.'

A rabbit uses its whiskers for tactile purposes (to touch), just as a cat does, e.g., finding its way in total darkness inside the burrow. There are also tactile hairs above the eyes; they signal to the animal when it has to pull in its head to avoid hitting an

Above: Rabbits have a highly developed sense of smell.

Opposite: A Netherland Dwarf. The whiskers and the long hairs above the eyes serve as sensors when the rabbit makes its way in the dark.

THE WORLD'S LARGEST SELECTION OF PET AND ANIMAL BOO

T.F.H. Publications publishes more than 900 books covering many hobby aspects (dc

. . . BIRDS . .

. . CATS . . .

. . . ANIMALS . . .

. . . DOGS . .

cats, birds, fish, small animals, etc.), plus books dealing with mo purely scientific aspects of the animal world (such as books abo fossils, corals, sea shells, whales and octopuses). Whether you are beginner or an advanced hobbyis you will find exactly what you're looking for among our complete listing of books. For a free catalo fill out the form on the other side of this page and mail it today. All T.F.H. books are recyclable.

Since 1952, *Tropical Fish Hobbyist* has been the source of accurate, up-to-the-minute, and fascinating information on every facet of the aquarium hobby. Join the more than 50,000 devoted readers worldwide who wouldn't miss a single issue.

overhead obstacle.

In contrast to the feet of such animals as dogs, cats, hamsters, and guinea pigs, the soles of rabbits' feet are covered by fur, from which only the long claws (used for digging and as 'spikes'

Above: Only when a rabbit spreads its toes can you see how long they are.

Opposite: The wrong way to pick up a rabbit. *Always* support the hindquarters when lifting a rabbit by its shoulder pelt.

for running) protrude. Because of the dense fur on the feet of rabbits, it is often overlooked that the toes (five on the front feet and five on the hind feet) are rather long, except the thumb on each front foot.

The long hind legs enable the rabbit to run

Above: This rabbit is bred for the quality of its fur.

Opposite: Female Belgian Hare.

fast; the short front legs keep the animal from falling forward onto its belly, in between each long leap. A rabbit's running power is contained in the hind legs, which essentially catapult the body forward. Therefore,

Above: Nothing is safe from a curious rabbit! Therefore, all elements of danger must be eliminated before the animal is let loose.

Opposite: This type of rabbit is bred for both its meat and fur.

hopping rabbits, can best be seen when the animal stretches its body. By the way, contrary to popular belief, rabbits can indeed move their hind legs independently. Otherwise, they could

rabbits and hares can run faster uphill than downhill, for downhill they would be doing somersaults with their long leaps! The true length of the legs, usually kept in an angled position in sitting or slowly

not groom themselves properly.

Of course, the front legs are not only a 'landing aid' between leaps, but they also serve other purposes. Rabbits use the front legs to burrow, to clean and

White New Zealands, male and female.

groom their face and ears, and to defend themselves. Feeding is done completely without the support of the front legs. The front legs are not used for holding.

The short tail is usually depicted in caricatures as being fluffy (cotton tail); however, a close examination reveals that only the underside of the tail is really fluffy. The top side of the tail is covered with shorter, body-colored hair. Normally the tail hangs down slightly so that only the outer, darker side can be seen. When a rabbit is excited, it raises its tail, and the white underside becomes a widely visible signal. This behavior is used during courtship, as well as in flight. Because of the hopping motion of a rabbit in full flight, this tail signal is particularly conspicuous.

Rabbit fur is relatively long. The outer guard hairs—unlike those of other fur-bearing

A rabbit and a stuffed hare. A rabbit is not to be treated as a toy; its fluffy mate is far better suited for that!

Netherland Dwarfs. The ideal weight for members of this breed is 2 1/2 pounds.

This pile shows how much fur
an adult Angora-type rabbit can
produce in one year.

animals—are soft; the
undercoat is, of course,
especially soft. Just touch
a rabbit, and you will
immediately become
aware of why these
animals are such popular
pets.

The fur is particularly
soft in the area between
the ears and at the onset
of the neck—which is the
spot where the rabbit
likes to be caressed by its
owner and touched by
other rabbits. In order to
direct the attention of
other rabbits to this spot,
the outer fur of this area
is rust-brown, while the
rest of the rabbit's body is
mostly grayish. Mutual
grooming is an activity in
which rabbits take great
delight.

FROM WILD ANIMAL TO DOMESTICATED PET

The place of origin of the European wild rabbit is the Iberian Peninsula and parts of North Africa. In fact, Spain is indebted to the 'long ear' for its name! When the Phoenicians reached the Iberian Peninsula, they noticed many small gray animals. These animals reminded them of a creature they knew from their home country, namely the cliff sleeper or, more accurately, the large-toothed hyrax (which looks a bit like a large guinea pig but is really a close relative of the ungulates [hoofed animals]). In their language, the cliff sleeper was called 'Shaphan,' and so they called this new country 'Isaphan,' country of the cliff sleepers. The Romans later colloquialized 'Hispania,' which eventually became 'Espana' or Spain, respectively. In essence then, Spain is the 'land of the rabbits!'

The usefulness of rabbits as a source of edible meat was already recognized by the

Romans, but field hares, as domestic animals, did not breed as prolifically and could be frightened too easily. Field hares were used to living in wide open spaces and when in full flight would simply break their necks

Below: In line with the original purpose of breeding rabbits as table meat, they were initially bred for size only.

Opposite: English Butterfly, male.

in those small pens ('leporariums') surrounded by solid walls. Thus, the Romans changed over to wild rabbits instead. Although rabbits tend to be flighty, they found security in their burrows dug inside the leporariums. In addition, they were prolific breeders.

By the way, it is still very difficult to acclimate a newly captured rabbit or hare to a life in pens or hutches unless it is a very young animal, and so it needs to be reared with formula feeding via a bottle. This makes us appreciate even more the early efforts by French monks and nuns who—during the early Middle Ages—attempted to domesticate the wild rabbit by using only

animals with a calm disposition as brood stock. The rabbit became the domesticated animal of the peasants; it was easy to feed, did not require much space, and supplied not only meat but also a soft-furred pelt. It stands to reason that even children at that time already had pet rabbits, but rabbits were still principally used to provide meat for the dinner table.

The main breeding objective was to produce larger and larger rabbits with a quiet disposition. Soon thereafter the first special breeds appeared.

Netherland Dwarfs are popular both as pets and as show animals.

In order to get pelts of uniform quality, rabbit breeders started to line-breed for particular color strains. One of the earliest of such color strains was the so-called Dutch rabbit, which is white with black ears, a large black circle around each

Above: The Dutch coloration is one of the oldest among domesticated rabbits.

Opposite: Electrical cable, wall paper, baseboards... a rabbit will give in to its gnawing instinct if you do not train it properly.

A broken fawn Holland Lop (senior buck).

Holland Lops are not quite as small as a true dwarf breed like the Netherland Dwarf, but some people opt for them because of their lovely loppy ears.

eye, and a black rump.

In Europe during the middle of the 12th century, wild rabbits continued to be kept in pens similar to the old Roman leporariums, purely for hunting purposes. This custom spread through France and on into England, where apart from pen maintenance, rabbits were also released on small islands and allowed to breed freely.

The first wild rabbits reached Germany about

Opposite: Rabbits love to nibble. These two youngsters are vying for a tender morsel of green. **Below:** Czechoslovakian Spotted.

1300 A.D. (actually *after* the domesticated rabbit!). As had been done successfully in England, the first rabbits were released on an island, the North Sea island of Amrum; from there the rabbits were moved eventually onto the mainland. From then on, escaped rabbits became quickly and firmly established throughout many parts of Europe.

Towards the end of the 18th century, the first long-haired (angora) rabbits and 'lop ears' started to appear among the domesticated rabbit populations. It was not until early this century that breeders began to rear animals that were particularly small; this was done essentially for

A direct comparison between a genuine and a false dwarf rabbit clearly shows the differences. The young mixed-breed miniature rabbit already has distinctly longer ears than the fully grown genuine dwarf on the left.

TRUE AND FALSE 'DWARFS'

The first dwarf type to be produced from domesticated rabbits was the ermine rabbit. (The ermine is a northern species of weasel that produces the much sought-after snow white pelt during the winter months.) Ermine rabbits are albinos, that is, they lack melanin and thus have red eyes and white fur. Yet, apart from the red-eyed animals, there have also been for some time now blue-eyed ermines (which are not true albinos); however, these are not often kept.

It must be pointed out here that the ermine rabbit is not simply a miniaturized hutch hare. Instead, it has totally

enjoyment and not to produce meat rabbits. It was from then on—by leaps and bounds—that the rabbit became an animal for the home—a pet!

different body proportions than its large relatives, which is the main reason for its tremendous popularity as a pet!

The extremely short head, which appears to be without a neck, is located directly on the animal's shoulders, giving it a chubby-faced appearance. Important characteristics are also the short ears, situated close together. The body is cylindrical, which gives the animal a rather compact shape. Even adult ermines seem like baby rabbits because of the roundish body dimensions; this tends to appeal very much to the human instinct of caring for and cuddling these cute animals.

Dutch breeders succeeded in producing colored dwarf rabbits by crossing ermines with large breeds. Today's dwarf rabbit types were established by further in-crosses with ermines. Therefore, strictly speaking, the colored dwarfs are nothing more than colored ermine rabbits.

Apart from these chubby standard-bred rabbits, which are often kept by breeders, there are other miniature rabbits that do not conform to established standards. While this may sound despairing it is really not intended to do that! Not being part of a standard breed means only that these animals do not exhibit pure-bred color patterns, and that there are also variations in size and body proportions. Therefore, we are dealing here not with a standard breed but indeed a non-standardized 'mixture,' which, however, can be

The fur of Angora-type rabbits is used for various items of clothing.

just as cute and cuddly as a rabbit from an established breed!

The only disadvantage of these non-uniform dwarf rabbits is the fact that their appearance often does not produce what it promises! As youngsters, they are often just as small as genuine dwarf rabbits, only to grow eventually much larger than had been expected! Yet, non-standard dwarfs can be recognized by the proportions of their bodies; usually they are much longer than real dwarfs. Invariably, the neck will be clearly visible, the head longer, and in particular the ears are not only longer but they are also spaced

Above: Californian, male.

Opposite: French Butterfly.

further apart. It is important to note very carefully the subtle difference between a colored dwarf and a miniaturized rabbit. Some newer breeds include the lop-eared (often just called lops) dwarf rabbit and the Angora dwarf rabbit.

As indicated by the name, lop-eared rabbits are those with long, droopy (hanging) ears.

Some years ago they too were systematically miniaturized, and today they are a distinct breed. Because of their somewhat melancholic look, lop-eared rabbits have found many fans.

Only in recent times have there been significant advances in the breeding of small angora rabbits. The first

Opposite: A male German Ram.

Below: A longhaired rabbit.

of these have already become available through pet shops.

COLORFUL DWARF VARIETIES

There are a number of color varieties and pelt markings among genuine dwarf rabbits, which will breed true in line-breeding; others are still being developed. There are black color varieties, wild-gray (like that of the original wild rabbit), blue, red, Havana (chestnut brown), chinchilla (a mixture of silver-gray, white and black hairs, which give a salt and pepper pattern), pearl miniver (bluish-gray with a slight brownish tinge).

There are also many distinct patterns of pelt markings. Martens show the color varieties brown and yellow (Siamese). These are the basic colors that always occur in

Opposite: A sable point Netherland Dwarf. **Above:** Female Russian Ermine.

conjunction with a darker face mask and an identically colored tail, ears and feet. Russian-colored dwarf rabbits are white with red eyes, yet have nose, ears, feet and tail that are either black or blue. Thuringer dwarfs have a chamois-yellow pelt with a sooty veil, which is rather prominent over ears, snout, cheeks, flanks and legs. This veil also extends from the snout to around the eyes and up to the ears.

Silver dwarfs have a base color of black or blue, with a white belly. The tail is also white below, as is the inside of the legs. In addition, the inside of the ears is just as white, as are the cheeks and the rings around eyes and nostrils.

Above: White Viennese.

Opposite: Diet is influential in the quality of a rabbit's coat.

Of particular attraction are the white-tipped guard hairs which create a silvery sheen over the pelt. The white to silvery gray triangular patch on the neck is also quite conspicuous in silver dwarfs.

Similar in appearance to silver dwarfs are the tan dwarfs. These have a

Above: A Netherland Dwarf buck. **Opposite:** A white
Netherland Dwarf. In this variety, the white color, ideally, should
be free of any yellow- or cream-colored tinge.

base color of black-tan or brown-tan. The white pelt areas (in silvers) are in these animals tan colored (a vivid yellow-red). However, chest and throat are solid colors and do not exhibit lighter shades, but this color pattern is not yet genetically fixed. A similar situation (of genetic instability) exists with the Japanese-colored dwarf, which could be described as being yellow with an asymmetrical (black) tiger pattern. Lop-eared dwarfs are bred in the same color varieties.

Among non-standard miniature rabbits one can frequently find pied varieties, which are rare among true colored or lop-eared dwarfs. These are very popular as pets.

Opposite: A male Burgundy rabbit.

Above: A smoke pearl Britannia Petite.

A lovely orange Netherland Dwarf doe.

A Rabbit in Your Home

Getting a pet, irrespective of what kind, must be a well-thought-through decision. Many spontaneously acquired pets are frequently dumped at the local animal pound only a few weeks or months later; or worse, they are simply released to fend for themselves. An animal is not a throw-away article!

Therefore, it is of immense importance to determine clearly before hand what the consequences are of getting a pet for yourself (and for your children!).

Each animal has a predetermined way of life, forced upon it by nature. It can deviate from this to a certain degree; this is known as adaptability. Of course, there is a difference between an animal living in the wild and one that lives among humans. The latter is spared the daily fight for survival in the wild. Yet, we humans must attempt

Before acquiring a pet dwarf rabbit, decide who in the family will be responsible for his daily care.

The food bowl must be heavy and secure, so that it does not tip over when the rabbit puts its front paws on the rim.

to provide the animal in our care with a natural way of life. In the case of our rabbits this does not mean that we have to cover our living room floor with garden soil and start sowing grass seeds! A suitable substitute is the logical answer: a rabbit can just as well scratch around the bedding on the floor of the hutch or pen, and food can be placed directly in front of its nose. It is important, however, to maintain its normal rest cycle, during which time it should not be disturbed. This prevents stress, which could dramatically reduce the natural life span of the animal. Children, especially, must be made aware of this requirement.

Small rations of fresh fruits and vegetables will help to keep your rabbit healthy.

If you are a chain smoker or if you listen every day to very loud music, you can not expect the animal to feel comfortable in your home. Similarly, if you are rarely at home you may also wish to reconsider getting a rabbit, because these are highly sociable animals—just like dogs—and they will quickly feel

Music played at concert-level volume is nothing more than a disturbing noise to the sensitive ears of a rabbit.

A tame rabbit enjoys nestling on the lap of its owner and being gently petted.

abandoned if there is nobody around to look after them regularly.

Do you like going on vacations? Please remember that you cannot simply take the animal along into foreign countries. Consequently, you have to provide substitute care for your long-eared pet. If it is your child who wants a rabbit for a

Children should be taught the right way to hold their pet rabbit: securely, but not too tightly.

pet, give detailed instructions on what is involved in proper animal care. Feeding, cleaning the cage and attending to all of the animal's needs must become part of the child's daily routine, just like doing school

Opposite: Netherland Dwarf.

Below: The more you handle your dwarf rabbit the more relaxed he will be in your presence.

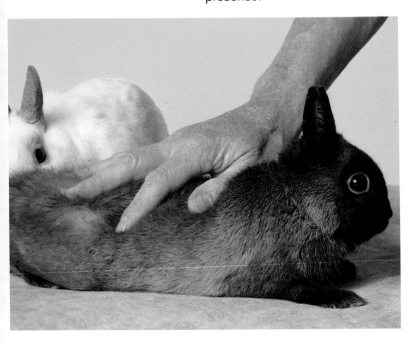

homework. Although a rabbit at home is a pet, it must never be looked upon as a toy; fluffy stuffed bunnies are more appropriate for that! You should also tell your child that a rabbit must not be treated as a

Above: Rabbits like a soft bed of hay; they like to burrow into it.

Opposite: A Himalayan Netherland Dwarf.

mindless object, so that the child is not surprised when 'Hoppie' sometimes bites or scratches when incorrectly handled.

For many self-appointed animal lovers, interest in the animal wanes rapidly when it turns out that it is too much trouble. It can happen that a rabbit refuses to be toilet-trained and constantly deposits his droppings on the carpet. Would this upset you? If it does, I strongly advise you against getting a rabbit as a pet!

You must also keep in mind that your pet rabbit may get sick and require proper attention. Should this happen, would you be willing to cancel a planned weekend trip if need be and also pay

If you are going to let your rabbit loose in your home, be prepared for the consequences. Rabbits will eliminate at will and not all can be litter trained.

veterinary fees that may be higher than what you have paid for the animal in the first place? In essence then, you will have to adapt to the needs of the animal; it cannot be the other way around! If you are unquestionably ready for all of this, only then

Above: Male Black-brown rabbit.

Opposite: The overall needs of a rabbit are small, compared to other kinds of pets, but your pet will still need regular daily attention.

A Netherland Dwarf peering out from the safe confines of his carrying basket.

should you go ahead and get a rabbit as a pet.

HOW LONG DOES A RABBIT LIVE?

In contrast to some other pets, a rabbit can get rather old. Unless there is inadequate care and lack of attention, and without an accident or serious illness, it is possible for a rabbit to reach an age of ten years or so. On the average, however, most rabbits kept as pets will not get much older than about seven years. Such longevity clearly exceeds that of such pets as hamsters, mice and rats. So there is much to be said for a rabbit as a pet for growing children. Both child and rabbit can

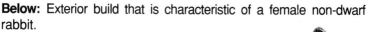

Below: Exterior build that is characteristic of a female non-dwarf rabbit.

grow up together, and there will not be a tearful instead will go on for seven or even ten years!

parting after two years or so (as, for instance, with pet hamsters). On the other hand, it also means that the daily duties of looking after the animal do not last two years only (already an incredibly long time span for a small child), but

Above: A trio of Netherland Dwarfs.

Opposite: The average lifespan of a rabbit is about seven years. However, this figure can vary from breed to breed.

Older rabbits are not as active as younger ones, and they need longer rest periods. As time goes on there will also have to be a change in the diet towards more readily digestible food. As painful as the death of a pet rabbit is to a child, use this to explain to your child about the mortality of all life! If gently and caringly explained, the death of a much-loved pet can be appropriate preparation for greater losses in later life. Teach your child about the first signs of old age in your rabbit, such as loss of weight and condition, slower movements and need for longer rest periods. Tell your child from that point on that he should enjoy every single day he can with the animal. Naturally, you should

make the animal as comfortable as possible during its declining years.

A rabbit that has become too weakened by old age generally just goes to sleep and one morning does not wake up. Tell your child that Hoppie is not afraid of dying and really enjoys its last few days; this removes much of the fear surrounding death. If possible, let the child or children properly bury the animal. If this cannot be done, quietly remove the dead animal and set up a simulated grave somewhere at a suitable site that you can show to your children later on. Please do not attempt to replace the deceased pet with a look-alike replacement, as children will notice the difference very quickly. Then, there is not only sadness about

Above: A young opal agouti Netherland Dwarf.

Opposite: A female Giant rabbit.

the lost pet but also disappointment about the deceitfulness of the parents!

YOUR RABBIT NEEDS COMPANY

By nature, rabbits are sociable animals. You should only get a single rabbit if you have enough time to play with it. One hour per day is about the minimum amount; however, the more the better. (Do not forget about rest periods.)

If you cannot devote quite that much time to a pet, you still will not have to do without a rabbit, just get...two! But remember that male rabbits (bucks) when they mature cannot get along with each other. On the other hand, if you get a true pair there will soon be little rabbits! Some hobbyists prefer to get two young females (adult females sometimes also have difficulties getting along with each other, unless they have grown up

Above: A Siamese smoke-pearl Netherland Dwarf.

Opposite: A dwarf-like rabbit in a watchful, defensive posture.

together). Another alternative is to get a very young pair, and then have the male castrated at the age of about four months. Not only will this minor operation inhibit future breeding, but it will also reduce the often unpleasant marking of territory, and the animal will become altogether much calmer. Yet, castrated rabbits have a tendency to put on weight, and so special attention must be paid to provide a well-balanced diet.

Even a totally different type of animal can sometimes be used as a companion for your pet rabbit. For instance, cats and dogs can sometimes make friends with a pet rabbit, but such friendship usually grows very slowly and should be constantly watched; after all, cats and dogs are, by nature, enemies of rabbits. Rabbits and guinea pigs are often kept together. If these two get along well, a very entertaining friendship will develop. Chinchillas can also make good playmates for pet rabbits.

Opposite: English Butterfly.

Above: If you are going to keep but a single rabbit, he must be given daily opportunities for play and exercise.

MALE OR FEMALE?

Whether a rabbit can be tamed or not is not dependent upon its sex; what matters is the individual nature of the animal and the way you handle it. Consequently, whether it is a female or a male is completely irrelevant for keeping rabbits as pets. Generally, the male is called a buck and the female is the doe. Male rabbits use a special method to mark their territory: they spray urine on what they consider to be their property and territory. This habit can be

Female Silver. The sex of a rabbit has no bearing on its ability to be tamed.

Like many other kinds of animals, rabbits can vary in their personality and temperament.

somewhat embarrassing when it occurs in your home. Castration will normally eliminate it, and spraying usually ceases after the operation. On the other hand, not every male rabbit sprays; unfortunately, you may not find out for certain until after you have taken the animal home. For instance, I once owned three males and none of them sprayed. If you get your pet from a rabbit breeder, sexing the animal is never a problem. Pet shops also

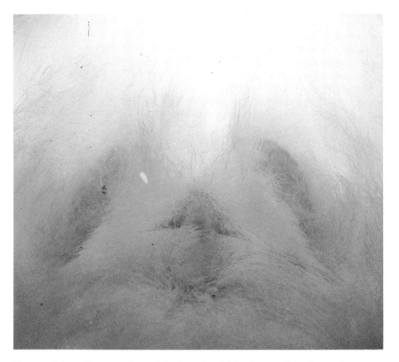

Determining the sex in adult dwarf rabbits is easiest in males. The naked testicles on either side of the genital opening are clearly visible.

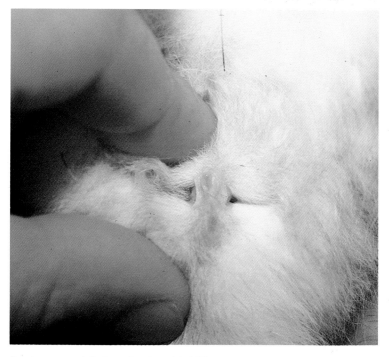

Sexing an adult female dwarf rabbit.

should be able to distinguish between a male and female rabbit. Occasionally, mistakes are made. Once I had a 'guaranteed' female called 'Diana,' but after a few weeks I had to change its name to 'Harvey' when it turned out to be a male. Such a mistake can, of course, be rather annoying when you thought you had acquired two females.

In order to determine the sex of your rabbit, place it on its back. It is important to hold the animal firmly so that it cannot scratch you or be inadvertently dropped when struggling to get free. Then, moisten the fur in the area of the sex organ, so that the hairs can easily be parted and you can get an unobstructed view. After that, you gently part the outer margin of the anal-genital region. In males, the anal as well as the genital openings are round, and there is a definite distance between them. The genital opening in females is slit-like, terminating towards the anal opening so that it appears as if both openings transcend into each other. In adult males the testicles are usually clearly visible.

Your pet shop dealer will be able to help you determine the sex of your rabbit.

A dwarf rabbit does not require spacious accommodations. Thus, it can make a suitable pet for the rabbit-loving apartment dweller.

Netherland Dwarf displaying the agouti coloration.

Dwarf rabbits are available in a wide array of lovely colors. If your pet shop dealer doesn't have the particular variety that you want, perhaps he can order it for you.

Buying and Transporting Your Pet

Naturally, many people think of their local pet shop as a source of dwarf rabbits. However, it is not always possible for your pet shop dealer to stock every variety of dwarf rabbit that is available. If that is the case, you may want to contact a dwarf rabbit breeder. Since a breeder is always determined to breed his animals as close to the breed standards as possible, he is generally very keen to dispose of those animals that deviate marginally from these standards; these can be rabbits with incorrect color patterns or possibly overly long ears, and so they are often sold at bargain prices. Addresses of breeders are available from local rabbit fancier clubs or appropriate journals and magazines.

Rabbits offered for sale in newspapers are sometimes fake dwarfs: these are rabbits that become too large and too difficult to handle. But there can also be exceptions. Sometimes, rabbits offered for sale in a newspaper can indeed

Above: Blue, blue-eyed white, and chocolate Netherland Dwarfs.

Opposite: A longhaired rabbit.

be very cute animals, which had to be disposed of for other reasons, such as a suddenly discovered allergy by the new owner, the arrival of a baby, job change and less spare time. It can be worthwhile to have a look at these rabbits, and sometimes it is love at first sight—even though the 'long-ear' may be slightly larger than that originally wanted. If a particular advertisement offers 'young rabbits for sale by breeder,' ask the breeder to show you the parents. That will give you an excellent indication of how large the young will eventually become—unless they are indeed pure-bred dwarf rabbits. Do not make a spontaneous decision. A bunch of cute little rabbits huddled together in a cage at a pet shop may indeed soften any heart, but it is imperative that the consequences of keeping a pet rabbit are well thought through. If this is not done, it may well happen that the animal care instinct— triggered at first sight of

A beautiful pair of Himalayan Netherland Dwarf rabbits.

A sable point Netherland Dwarf. In this variety, an ideal
specimen exhibits a very rich sepia color on the ears, nose, feet,
and tail.

A blue Netherland Dwarf. A healthy rabbit will be alert and attentive to his surroundings.

the cute little animal—may become extinguished just as quickly. A rabbit must never be a surprise present! There is no way you can anticipate how the recipient is going to react. Even if your child wants a rabbit and you want to fulfill his or her wish, the child should be permitted to select its own pet. All you should do ahead of time is get the cage and all other essential equipment and set it up. Then, the next day or so, take your child to a pet shop or rabbit breeder. To your surprise, you may discover that your child may immediately pick a particular rabbit that you would not have selected. This way, you prevent your offspring from wanting the pet rabbit from your next-door neighbor, rather than the one you would have picked out. A child will develop far stronger ties to an animal he or she has selected personally, because it is indeed his or her animal, rather than only a present from the parents!

In conclusion, a final remark. When I referred to 'breedless rabbits,' this was not meant to denigrate, but merely intended to refer to (possibly) over-sized animals. A breedless animal may not be worth much in monetary terms, but it can very much become a priceless pet. Just remember all those mixed-breed dogs that bring much joy to their owners, even though they have turned out somewhat differently

Himalayan Netherland Dwarf rabbit. This color variety gets its name from the Himalayan rabbit (a standard-sized rabbit).

from what they were as pups. I personally enjoyed my non-pedigreed rabbits just as much as the pure-bred ones; and if they did not remain quite as small as I had anticipated, I never worried about it!

Make sure the cage has a sufficiently high tray. It protects the animal against wind drafts and also stops much of the bedding from falling out of the cage.

WHAT TO LOOK FOR

Just as with any other pet, it is important to select a healthy animal. In doing so, it is equally important to look closely at all other animals in the same pen or enclosure, as well as closely scrutinize the rest of the

Genuine dwarf rabbits are available from pet shops or specialist breeders. Animals with minor flaws are often slightly cheaper.

pet shop's or breeder's facilities. Generally, unclean surroundings can enhance the development of parasites and the outbreak of diseases. Do not buy a rabbit that lives in a hutch or cage where the

Opposite: An example of a rabbit with psoroptic ear mange and the mite (*Psoroptes cuniculi*) that caused it.

Below: Baby dwarf rabbits, with their large, round heads and nubby little ears, are among the cutest of all baby animals.

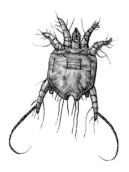

soiled bedding has obviously not been changed for a while. Responsible breeders and pet shop owners maintain the required hygienic standards. Decaying food and a urine-soaked "lavatory corner" in the cage are definite warning signs!

A healthy rabbit has bright clear eyes, a smooth shiny coat, and a dry nose. Discharge from the nose or the eyes are warning signs, as are scaly or bare patches anywhere on the body. Red, swollen eyelids are

An example of a rabbit with infectious stomatitis.

A Russian veterinary doctor and nurse performing a clinical examination on a rabbit.

symptoms of an eye infection. The area around the anal region must not be coated with sticky fecal matter. (However, a dry fecal pellet occasionally can become stuck, which is nothing to worry about.)

Small-bodied angora hybrids have emerged from the rabbit hobby in recent years.

This rabbit is suffering from an illness known as infectious rhinitis. Note the copious nasal discharge.

You must never buy an animal that shows signs of swelling inside the sensory openings. Such an animal may have contracted the rabbit disease myxomatosis;

A rabbit with infectious rhinitis will repeatedly rub its nose with its paws, thus causing the fur on the paws to become matted.

few animals ever survive it. Healthy rabbits are alert and curious; their movements are fluent and elastic. A bent back with a protruding vertebral column, together with unsure, awkward movements and general listlessness, are signs of disease or old age.

Sometimes it is difficult to distinguish between a resting rabbit and one that is ill; both will be hunched-up in a corner with their eyes partially or completely closed. However, healthy animals generally open their eyes immediately and perk up their ears as soon as the cage door is opened. If there is no response, then try to push the animal gently over to one side. A healthy animal will then

A rabbit exhibiting the symptoms of myxomatosis.

Opposite: Before giving birth, the female prepares a nest by mixing its own chest fur with the bedding. This behavior may also be a sign of false pregnancy.

Above: This rabbit's bent front paws could likely be a symptom of rickets.

A pair of sable marten Netherland Dwarf bucks. Can you tell
which one is shedding?

Front leg angulations: correct, bowlegged, splayed.

Rear leg angulations: correct, broad, narrowed.

immediately wake up and jump off to run away or actively push against your hand, like a stubborn mule. But if the rabbit can easily be nudged around without offering any resistance (it may even lose its balance), then you must refrain from the purchase, no matter how cute the animal may be. Well-healed wounds do

Above: Five-day-old dwarf rabbits.

Opposite: This rabbit is showing signs of paralysis of the hind region of its body.

not pose any danger to the health of the rabbit. On the other hand, large, festering wounds provide an open door for subsequent infections.

Above: This rabbit has the skin disease ringworm, which can be passed on to humans. **Opposite:** The top rabbit has a notoedric infestation. Next to it is the mite that carries the disease. The lower illustrations show a rabbit with a sarcoptic infestation and the mite that causes the condition.

This rabbit is suffering from coccidiosis, an infection of the digestive tract caused by a parasite.

BRINGING YOUR NEW PET HOME

No matter how tempting it may be to hold the cuddly little animal on your lap during the trip home, it should be carried in a darkened transport box or crate, with sufficient air holes punched in the sides and top. The trauma of having been dragged out of the cage and forced to leave its mates behind has already caused enormous stress to the animal. Moreover, the impressions of totally new surroundings cause added fears for the rabbit. All this may make it much more difficult for the animal to adjust to and accept humans. A dark transport box, however, offers the comforts of a burrow, where the rabbit can gradually adapt to new sounds and different odors. On the way home, the carrying box must be protected against rain and drafty conditions; it should also be kept out of the sun. Talking softly to the animal will also keep it calm.

Even after the rabbit has adjusted to its new home, a suitable transport

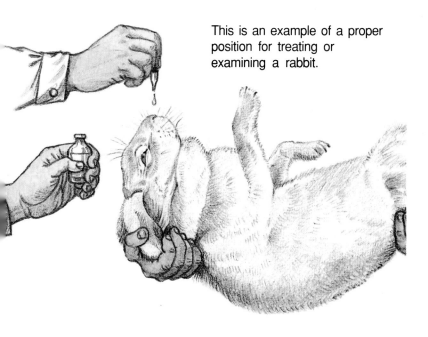

This is an example of a proper position for treating or examining a rabbit.

Sexing a rabbit requires that the animal's genitals be fully visible. However, do not let the rabbit dangle in midair. Place it on a firm surface and then lift up its backside.

This is the correct method for carrying adult rabbits.

box should always be readily accessible, for instance, for emergency trips to the veterinarian! By then, the original transport box may well be too small, since you will have used it to carry a baby rabbit home. Therefore, it is advisable to have a larger box or crate handy, or—ideally—a lockable carrier, as is used for small dogs and cats.

A solid transport box is not only useful for taking the animal home but also comes in handy for visits to the veterinarian.

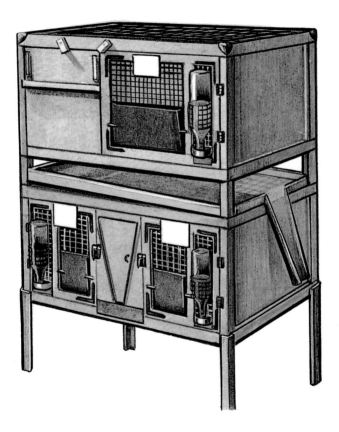

A specialized cage for rabbit farms. The top section is for the whelping female and her babies (up to 2 months). The lower section enables you to separate the babies from the mother.

Home for a Rabbit

It has already been suggested that the cage for the new pet must be on hand before the animal is actually purchased. At the same time, you should also start thinking about a suitable place for it in your home. (I should note here that in the remainder of this book, I am making the assumption that the rabbit is going to be kept in a house or apartment, rather than in a garden or on a balcony.)

CAGE LOCATION

Accommodating the cage in the kitchen is not a good idea! Apart from obvious implications for human hygiene and sanitary conditions (who wants rabbit hair in their soup?), the rattling of pots and pans will disturb the animal. After all, a rabbit's hearing is much better than that of humans! Moreover, cooking odors may also affect the rabbit's health and longevity.

Since a rabbit is mainly active during the day, it does not make any undue noise at night, so that it can be kept in a play room or den or even in a bedroom. In the case

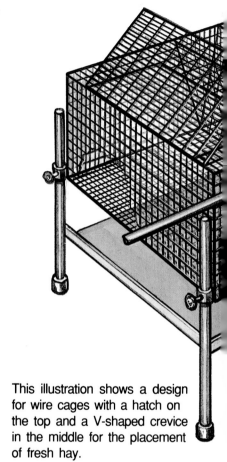

This illustration shows a design for wire cages with a hatch on the top and a V-shaped crevice in the middle for the placement of fresh hay.

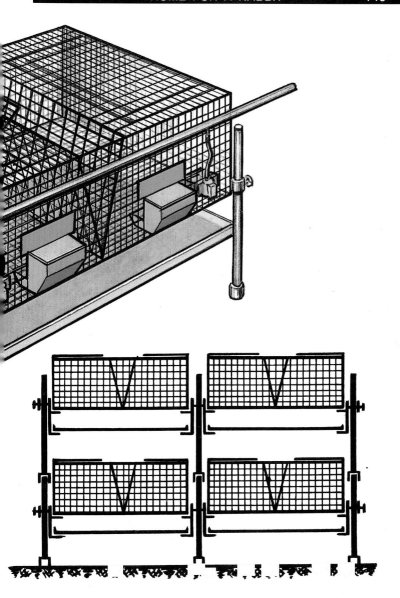

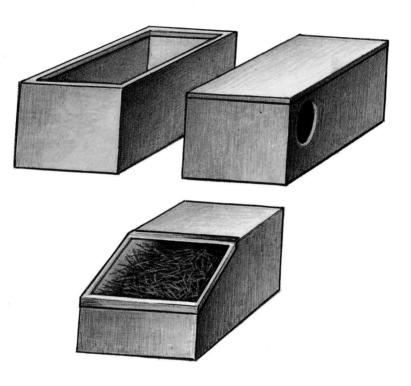

Above: An assortment of rabbit nest boxes.

Opposite: A wire crate or exercise pen makes a convenient temporary holding area, for example, when your pet's regular cage is being cleaned.

of the latter, there is no one to keep the animal company during the day, so the most suitable location for a rabbit cage is either a play room or the living room. As far as noise is concerned, rabbits are among the quietest of pets and will not disturb the neighbors. Occasionally, some rabbits—especially the larger ones—take up the habit of playing with their food dish, mainly by dragging it around, in order to attract attention. The animal most likely wants to be fed or simply wants someone to play with. Should this happen, it is advisable to look in on the animal because the constant rattling noise can be distracting (and even disturb the neighbors).

A pet does not belong in a room where there is a lot of smoking.

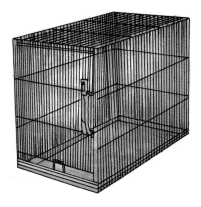

Similarly, loud noises hurt the rabbit's sensitive ears and will cause the animal to suffer stress. Even loud music—be it rock or classical music at concert volume—is perceived as painful noise. If there is a pet rabbit in the living room, use earphones if you need a 'sound experience!' Never put the cage near loudspeakers or near the television set.

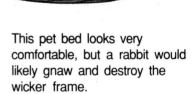

This pet bed looks very comfortable, but a rabbit would likely gnaw and destroy the wicker frame.

A rabbit's cage should never be exposed to direct sunlight. Although rabbits in the wild like to sun themselves, window panes act like a magnifying glass. At least part of the cage must always remain in the shade. Draft is also a serious health hazard for a rabbit. An ideal location is one where the cage is protected along one or two sides by a wall; this affords the animal some cover, whereas in a free-standing cage the animal feels less secure since it is constantly being watched.

A cage must be placed on a solid, firm support. In apartments with a concrete floor, the cage should be set on a suitably cut piece of styrofoam to keep out the cold from beneath.

This type of carrier not only provides good ventilation but also enables the occupant to see what is going on around him.

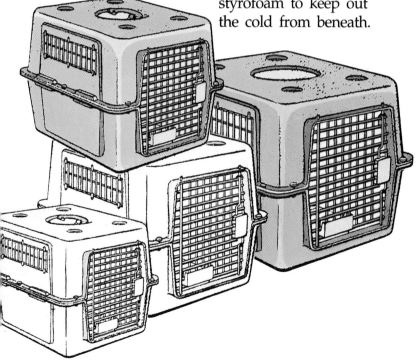

THE PROPER CAGE

Pet shops have a large variety of cages for sale. In order to make the correct selection, you

As I noted earlier, rabbits—whether they are a genuine breed or just simply a mixed, non-standard variety—grow

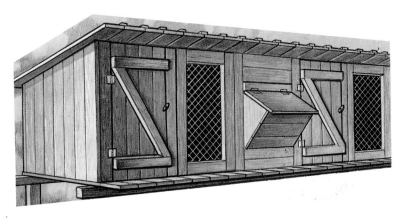

A rabbit cage designed in Russia. It is made of maple wood, with the front wall 78cm high and the back wall 56cm high.

have to consider the size, height of bottom tray, ventilation, wire mesh and accessibility for maintenance.

There are many cages being offered for keeping dwarf rabbits. (Some are really only suitable for guinea pigs.)

to different sizes and so their space requirements vary substantially. The rule of thumb for the smallest acceptable cage is that the rabbit must be able to stretch out with its entire body along one of the short sides of the cage; this

A Siamese sable Netherland Dwarf buck. (Note the excessively long claws, which should be clipped.)

measurement is then doubled for the long side of the cage. As far as the height is concerned, the rabbit must be able to sit up comfortably. Now, you must remember that you would normally purchase a young (baby) animal, and if it is a mixed breed, you will not even know how large such an animal gets. Therefore, once again in real measurements, a suitable home for a pet rabbit should be about 80 x 40 x 40 cm. Remember, the larger the better. If you want to keep two rabbits, or a rabbit and a guinea pig, the minimal dimension for the front of the cage should be one meter. Also, keep in mind that these dimensions are only applicable if the animal

is being let out regularly. If rabbits are kept too confined and they do not get regular exercise outside the cage, they will rapidly put on weight and then become listless. Such animals will rarely ever live to an old age.

Unless vacuuming the floor is one of your favorite pastimes, you must make sure that the cage comes with a high bottom tray. Bedding and strands of hay always fall out, as well as the odd fecal pellet. And when the rabbit gets a fright and executes the

Opposite: A Siamese Netherland Dwarf. All rabbits have highly developed senses of seeing and hearing.

proverbial 'jack rabbit start,' there will be a virtual shower of bedding, hay, etc. A tray of at least 10cm in height will contain much of the cage litter or at least restrict it to a small area around the cage.

Cages are available with wire-mesh screens; others are made completely out of plastic. Even an actively digging and scratching rabbit will not be able to throw out any rubbish from a plastic cage. However, plastic cages

tend to restrict ventilation and do not permit the urine to drain off. Moreover, these cages can get extremely hot in the summer, since ventilation can take place only across a small mesh window on top of the cage. These plastic cages also inhibit contact between animal and humans; one cannot even scratch the animal through the wire if there is not time to take the animal out of its cage. For the animal, it will be like sitting inside a

Rabbits can be great companions for people of all ages.

Rabbits are as clean as cats and spend a lot of time grooming themselves.

telephone booth! I also advise against keeping rabbits in old aquarium tanks and terrariums, again for reasons of poor ventilation in such enclosures. The good old wire cage is still the most suitable home for a pet rabbit.

In recent years, the mesh around some rabbit cages has been made of plastic-coated wire. Even though this makes for an attractive appearance, there is the disadvantage that the plastic is applied to a dark (metal) base color. If your rabbit has the tendency to chew on the wire front (which it usually does only out of boredom!) the colored plastic coating comes off and an ugly spotted pattern appears. The brighter the mesh, the more conspicuous it becomes. Since brightly colored mesh (because of its light-reflecting properties) already distracts from seeing the animal properly, I recommend—based on my own experience—the use of dark-coated wire mesh. Colors available include black, dark brown, dark blue and green. Pink and sky-blue may indeed be pretty (after all, the rabbit does not care what color its

Above: Ears pointing forward, a rabbit approaches the human hand or any unfamiliar object.

Opposite: Male black shorthaired rabbit.

cage is), but you do not want to look at the cage but rather at its occupant.

SERVICE ACCESS

The important consideration here is whether the cage has a door along its front panel or whether the entire roof can be lifted up. The advantages and disadvantages of both cancel each other out, but for the sake of completeness they should be mentioned. A front door enables the rabbit to jump in and out of the cage by itself (it does not have to be lifted out). With only the roof removable, you will have to lift the rabbit out of the cage or take the entire cage off its tray. On the other hand, the cage's interior is more readily accessible when the roof can be removed (and you do not have to crawl on your hands and knees to remove leftover food). For that reason, I tend to favor a cage with a removable (flip-top) roof.

BUILDING YOUR OWN CAGE

With all the sturdily designed commercial

This cage is designed to allow for two different floors—a permanent wire floor as well as a removable wooden one.

cages available, your best bet is to *purchase* a cage for your rabbit. If, however, you opt to

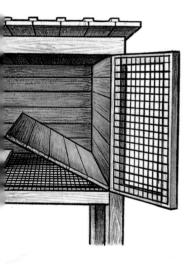

build a cage yourself, there are a few points to keep in mind. The best material to use is sheets of white plastic-coated chip board, masonite or similar material, as used for making kitchen furniture. This material is water-proof, easily cleanable and smooth, which prevents rabbits from getting a grip on it with their gnawing teeth. Any building material supplier will cut the sheet to any required dimensions. Building the cage yourself offers the possibility to optimize the utilization of available space. Once I had a small open space between two pieces of furniture, into which I had to fit a cage 1.2 m long. The cage was to hold a medium-sized rabbit, as well as a guinea pig.

The first thing I did was to make a crate

1.20 x .50 x .60m out of
sheets of chip board cut
to size; these sheets were
screwed together, leaving
an opening towards the
front. So that urine could
not soak into the joints, I
sealed them with silicon.

Along the front—at the
bottom—I attached a
15cm-high board that
was to prevent bedding
from falling out. All
visible open-cut edges on
the masonite were then
sealed properly, which

Opposite: A practical cage unit for young rabbits. Note the useful flip-top lid feature.

Above: Head shape characteristic of a female non-dwarf rabbit.

Above: Head shape characteristic of a male non-dwarf rabbit.

Opposite: This rabbit exhibits exterior build characteristics of a non-dwarf male.

gave the cage a more attractive appearance. I made two wooden door frames and attached the hinges. Then I selected black plastic-coated wire mesh—spot-welded into 14mm square mesh—which is commercially available for the construction of bird aviaries. This wire mesh is thin and strong, but it still gives sufficient visual penetration, since it is not glossy. I stapled the mesh onto the two door frames and attached a bolt to properly secure the doors. The completed cage looked elegant and it was practical.

By opening one or both of the doors I could let the animals out. At the same time, the cage was sufficiently high for the rabbit to sit up, and I did not have to crawl on my hands and knees to clean out leftover food. Soiled bedding was removed by means of an old scraper. Of course, I

could have also built in a tray, but that would have complicated the entire structure. Additionally, more bedding falls on the floor when pulling out a tray than when a scraper is used.

BEDDING

First you put newspaper down on the bottom of the cage; this will soak up any moisture. On this you place a layer of commercially available small animal bedding, which consists mainly of wood shavings. You could also get these, of course, from a carpenter, but you could not be sure whether the shavings have come from chemically treated

With the wide variety of rabbit food and bedding material that is available, it is unnecessary to offer evergreens.

Male Black-fire rabbit.

wood. There could also be foreign objects in it, like screws or metal splinters. Cat litter can also be used, but this is not quite soft enough for rabbits; their feet can develop sores. Yet, cat litter is excellent for soaking up urine. Saw dust is totally useless.

Peat moss is sometimes suggested for use as rabbit bedding, but I do not recommend it to be used in indoor housing. Often, bits of peat moss cling to the rabbit's fur, and it is then dragged through the entire room or apartment.

A PLACE TO SLEEP

At bedtime, the rabbit likes a corner with straw or hay. A regular sleeping box is normally not required, yet many animals will readily accept it (young animals, especially, feel very secure in it). Fully grown rabbits are sometimes too large for commercial

Clean rags can serve as a useful *temporary* bedding material.

Male Marburg Squirrel rabbit.

sleeping boxes, and so some hobbyists use a carton with a door cut out as a substitute. If your rabbit accepts a sleeping box, it will most certainly also use the top as a look-out. Therefore, if you use a carton substitute, make sure it is made out of strong cardboard, otherwise it may collapse under the weight of the animal or even tip over with the animal in it! Even a simple board attached from side to side inside the cage can provide a suitable roof.

THE RABBIT TOILET

Most rabbits are very clean, always using the same corner in their cage or hutch as a toilet; only the odd fecal pellet is dropped here and there! This characteristic can make it easy to house-train a rabbit. If your pet conforms to this behavior, then you can place cat litter into the corner selected by the animal; this tends to absorb wetness and odor more effectively than sawdust.

I went one step further with the cage I built myself: I placed an open 'cat box' in one corner. In the box I put a thick layer of newspaper and on top of that a layer of cat litter. Both

animals then used that tray to urinate, and the rabbit even deposited its fecal pellets there; however, the guinea pig tended to deposit its droppings at random throughout the cage. Once the animals had established this 'toilet

Rabbit chew-sticks will keep your pet occupied and satisfy its gnawing instincts.

regimen,' all I had to do was to regularly remove and clean the toilet tray, while the rest of the cage needed to be cleaned only once every two or three weeks.

FOOD AND WATER CONTAINERS

It is important for a rabbit to have a hay rack with a continuous supply of fresh hay. Hay used for bedding is unsuitable as food since it is usually wet from urine. If there is no fresh hay, a rabbit will feed on bedding hay, but this can lead to health problems. Young rabbits often like to jump up on the hay rack to get a better look around; this then tends to soil the feed hay also. Therefore, it is advisable to attach the hay rack as closely as possible to the wire mesh overhead. It is good for a rabbit to stretch itself a little as it reaches for the food. There are also half-round, basket-like racks which must be opened up to be filled, and the rabbit cannot jump on top of such a rack.

on them and can then easily swallow bits of plastic; this may have fatal consequences! It is important that the bowl be very heavy, since rabbits have the habit of

Grain and pelletized foods should be offered in a heavy porcelain or earthenware bowl. I strongly advise against using plastic bowls, since rabbits will chew

Female Butterfly rabbit.

Every cage should contain a rack of fresh hay that is changed regularly.

placing their front feet on the edge of the bowl while feeding; this could easily tip over the feed bowl unless it is sufficiently heavy.

There is no need for a green food container; this food is simply

Above and opposite: These illustrations show a slightly different way to style the placement of the feeder and water dispenser in your homemade cage.

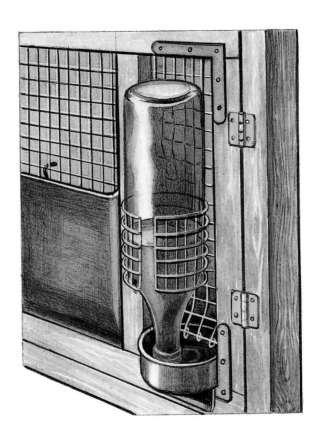

placed on the bedding (but *not* in the toilet corner). Using a bowl for drinking water is not a good idea. Rabbits tend to step in it, or manage to get bedding or fecal pellets into it, or even tip it over. Water is most suitably offered via a rabbit drinking bottle. This is a bottle with a narrow pipe and a small inert ball at the end, which dispenses drops of water on demand (i.e., when the animal licks it).

OTHER CONSIDERATIONS

When a rabbit runs on bedding—or on carpet, when let out of its cage— that is, when it moves constantly on soft substrates, our pet is not grinding its claws down sufficiently. Eventually they will protrude beyond the end of the foot and ultimately hinder the animal in its normal activities; long claws may even become painful to the rabbit. In order to avoid frequent visits to a veterinarian to get the claws trimmed

Commercially available rabbit food mixtures contain all essential ingredients for proper nutrition.

back—a trip your pet distinctly dislikes—you just place a sandstone tile in the middle of the cage. In its normal movements through the cage, such as getting from the sleeping corner to the feed bowl, the rabbit always has to transverse this tile. The rough surface texture of the sandstone tile will keep the growth of the rabbit's claws in check. When the animal is being let out, just place the tile (which can also be an ordinary footpath tile) outside the cage door, so that the rabbit has to move across it. By the way, on very hot summer days rabbits like to cool their 'tummy' on these tiles!

THE OUTDOOR RUN

This book is intended primarily for those animal lovers who would like to keep one or two rabbits in a house or apartment. (City dwellers especially like to keep a dwarf rabbit, particularly when the landlord does not permit a dog or cat in the apartment.) There is really no opportunity to keep a rabbit outdoors when one lives in the city, and so this topic is not discussed at length; moreover, there are topical books on this subject.

Keeping a rabbit on a balcony presents problems that must be taken into consideration. Many balconies are too drafty, the floor is too cold or there is no shade; city life adds exhaust

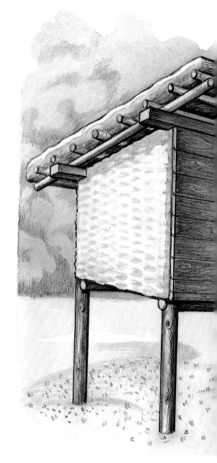

Outdoor housing must be elevated off the ground to protect its occupants from predators.

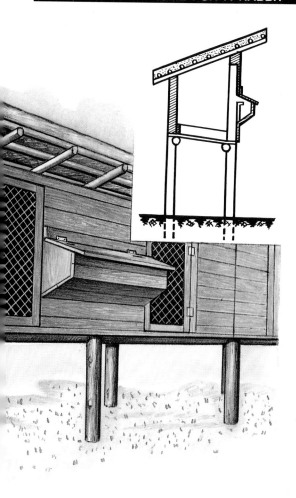

fumes and street noise. Consequently, take the animal outside only when the weather is mild and then only for an hour. Place the cage on something that insulates the animal against the cold coming up from the concrete floor (e.g., a sheet of styrofoam), and make sure there is no direct

Opposite: This style of housing shows bricks as a main support structure and the use of a thatched-style roof.

Below: This cage includes an enclosed shelter and open-air section, in which the rabbit has plenty of room to roam about.

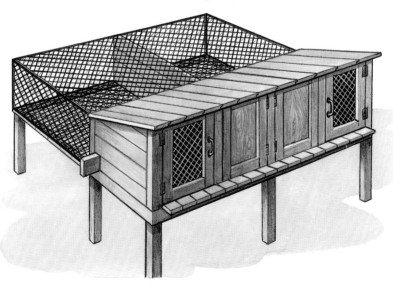

exposure to the sun. Giving the animal a run in the park is, of course, only possible if you put it on a leash. For that purpose, do not use a collar. Use a chest harness instead, as is used for small dogs or cats. The leash only prevents the animal from escaping; a rabbit will never learn to 'heel.' You have to let it hop wherever it wants to go and you follow it on the leash!

Opposite: Black Netherland Dwarf. **Above and below right:** Tattooing a rabbit's ear for identification purposes.

There are, however, serious dangers in such excursions, especially in a city. Your rabbit may nibble on plants that may have been sprayed with insecticides or are covered by exhaust fume deposits. If it comes into contact with bird or dog droppings, it can pick up diseases or such parasites as canine

tapeworms. Finally, free-roaming dogs can hurt your rabbit or cause it to virtually die of fright. Therefore, if you are not one of the lucky ones who lives in the country, or at least in the suburbs, it is better to keep your pet indoors. With sufficient exercise, it will be quite happy!

Opposite: Himalayan Netherland Dwarf. **Below:** A lovely mixed breed.

A short stay on the balcony does not hurt the rabbit, but what about the balcony plants. . .?

The Correct Diet

Rabbits are true vegetarians and refuse all meaty supplements. Although your pet rabbit's menu is variable, it does not contain any specialized items. And so, feeding a rabbit properly is child's play. A proper diet is one that is well balanced. Apart from proteins, a rabbit requires lots of roughage, so that digestion functions correctly. Even though a rabbit is undemanding, it should not become a consumer of leftovers. A rabbit's body can react very adversely to certain food items consumed by humans. A balanced diet consists of the correct amounts, as well as proper diversity. This is an essential prerequisite for a healthy pet!

GENERAL FEEDING RULES

Please do not rely on the rabbit to select only those foods that are good for it! A wild rabbit may have this sort of instinct, but this is largely absent in its domesticated cousin.

Green food that you have collected yourself must not have come from areas adjacent to factories or busy motorways. All fruit and vegetables must be thoroughly washed. Even guaranteed organically grown vegetables and fruit can carry bird droppings, which may contain salmonella. Moreover, self-collected green food can come from an area where myxomatosis is prevalent. Meticulous washing of all food items is the best and only effective precaution a rabbit owner can take.

All green food that has been washed must be well drip-dried. Do not feed grass and other plants wet with dew; this can make your

Opposite: Netherland Dwarfs. The basic staple in a rabbit's diet is a commercial pellet mix.

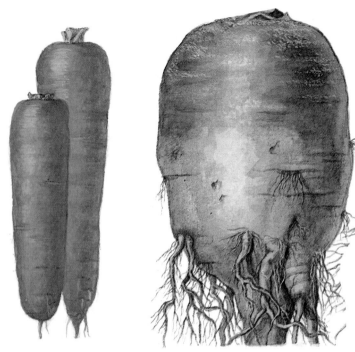

Carrots (left) and swedes, or rutabagas, (right) are two vegetables that are acceptable for your rabbits to eat.

rabbit very sick. If your rabbit has not had fresh green food for a while, it must get used to it again but gradually. You have to be particularly careful with newly weaned animals that have never tasted green food. Start out with very small portions, and then gradually increase the quantities. Carrots, the proverbial rabbit food, act as a laxative if given in excessive amounts.

DAILY FOOD RATIONS

The rabbit is a creature of habit and likes to get its meals every day at the same time. The amount it gets depends, of course, on its size; as I have pointed out repeatedly, not every dwarf rabbit remains a dwarf! The following quantities, however, are applicable only to genuine dwarf rabbits and other small breeds.

For breakfast, your rabbit should have a handful of rabbit-mix pellets (that is about 20 to 30 g). In the afternoon, we give green food, just enough so that all of it is eaten immediately. At the beginning it is better to cut this ration a bit short and then gradually increase it to the correct quantity. It is difficult for me to give you the correct amounts in grams or carrot-centimeters, but 1/8 of an average-sized apple is sufficient per day. Fresh hay, items to chew, and fresh drinking water (renewed daily) must

Do not feed your rabbits potatoes of any kind.

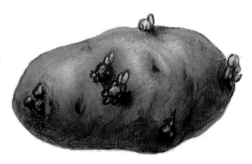

always be available to your pet.

READY MIXED FOODS

The basic staple diet for rabbits should be a ready mix, available from pet shops. It consists of various types of grain and the so-called pellets. The latter are quite small, cylinder-shaped and consist of compressed ingredients of greenish to greenish brown color. Among other things, they contain nutritionally important vitamins, minerals and trace elements. In terms of

Opposite: Male gray Giant rabbit. **Above:** This is a rounded feeder, which enables several rabbits to eat from the same bowl at the same time.

their ingredients, pellets are completely sufficient as a basic food item for rabbits. Rabbit breeders purchase their pellets in large quantities. You may also wish to do that since pellets are available in 10 lb. bags. Make sure you buy the type of pellet used for rearing and not for fattening rabbits! After all, you are not rearing your pet for the cooking pot; you only want to keep it in top condition.

Even though pelleted rabbit food is nutritionally complete and practical, it does have one disadvantage, namely that after a while the animal can get bored with it. Eating is more than just a mechanical way of staying alive, not only for humans, but also for animals. Desire and appetite are very much a part of eating—for the rabbit too.

Therefore, a single-type of balanced basic food is good, but it is even better when supplemented with other nutritional ingredients. Even the nutritionally balanced grain feeds can be further enhanced with occasional supplements. The operative word here is 'occasional,' because when given regularly, even a choice tidbit becomes boring! From my own experience, I can recommend the following basic food items: oatmeal (present in some mixtures, or replaced with a similar cereal), corn flakes, and various crisp breads and crackers. In addition, some food manufacturers also offer a variety of 'munchies,' such as yogurt candy, vegetable crackers and other items.

Opposite: Cabbage and all of its varieties can cause diarrhea, or scours, in rabbits.

Greenfoods such as beets should be given only in small quantity.

animals. Sometimes an animal will starve before it accepts a certain type of food. Take a sample of the food which your rabbit was given at the breeder's or pet shop when you go out to buy more food for your pet. If you change the brand, do this slowly and deliberately: mix some of the old food with the new one, and then gradually lessen the quantity of old food. This approach lessens the dangers of digestive problems.

In contrast to other pets, it is hardly worthwhile to mix your

Please keep in mind that some animals are individualists! Not all rabbits like the same foods or particular food ingredients; sometimes there has to be some experimentation in order to determine the food preference of particular

Opposite: An assortment of edible wild plants: dandelion (left), mallow (right), and plantain (bottom).

own rabbit food.
Mixtures available from
pet shops are
nutritionally well-
balanced and are eagerly
eaten by most rabbits.
Nevertheless, if you are
determined to do this,
get yourself the
previously mentioned
ingredients, the pellets as
well as the following
cereals: corn, oats, barley
and wheat. With these
ingredients on hand you
can prepare a
nutritionally balanced—
and for your rabbit,
interesting—diet. Please
your pet by periodically
varying the mix ratios,
and it will reciprocate
your extra efforts by
being active and staying
in good health.

ROUGHAGE

Rabbits must have
constant access to fresh
hay as so-called
roughage; this is
essential for proper
digestion. Hay must be
stored dry and
ventilated, in order to
inhibit mold growth
(which could be
dangerous for your long-
eared pet). Correctly
stored hay smells
pleasant and spicy;
spoiled hay has a musty
odor and must then not
be used as feed. It should
also not be used for
bedding, since most
rabbits nibble on the odd
straw from their own
bed. Your pet shop sells
hay in bags, or you can
get it by the bale from
any feed store or farmer.
Straw is only used for
bedding, *never* as food.

OTHER FOODS

The types and
ingredients of foods just

Rabbits enjoy nibbling on alfalfa (left) and red clover.

Pictured left to right: a wild radish, an ornamental poppy, and a variety of mustard. None are poisonous.

Horsetail (left) and hedge nettles (all varieties) are not edible wild plants.

mentioned are essential to a well-balanced rabbit diet. Although rabbits are not rodents (in zoological terms), they are just as eager in their hunt for food as are rodents. Wild rabbits, for instance, do not only munch on grasses and dandelions but also gnaw on the bark of bushes and trees (as every gardener and forester knows only too well). For this sort of feeding, our rabbit has been equipped with chisel-like incisor teeth. These are unlike our own teeth, inasmuch as they do not have typical roots, and so they grow continuously. If rabbits are not afforded an opportunity to gnaw and so to wear these teeth down, the incisors would get longer and longer and eventually protrude from the mouth. This would clearly interfere with normal feeding and a rabbit with such misformed teeth would surely starve to death in the wild. Domesticated rabbits with such tooth problems can be treated by a veterinarian, who will snip off overly long incisors; yet, early prevention is better than a late treatment.

Therefore, it is important that rabbits always have something hard to chew on to keep busy, such as old (dried)

Opposite: Buffalo bur (left) and foxglove, both of which are poisonous.

bread (must not be moldy) or branches from leafy trees, especially from fruit trees (these must not have been sprayed!). If there is nothing to gnaw on, your rabbit will attempt to satisfy this urge on your furniture. This must not be interpreted as destructiveness, but rather a natural response to an innate instinct!

Pet food manufacturers offer a number of special feeds for that purpose, in which the pleasant (choice tidbit) is combined with the essential (gnawing food). There are various brands and types of cracker-like products that generally contain a soft wooden center encased in a layer of grains and certain tasty bits; some are merely firmly compressed food. The nutritional analogy of this food (to that of humans') is the bag of popcorn or chips that one consumes while watching television, except that it is much healthier for rabbits.

GREEN FOODS

The term 'green food' includes fruit, vegetables and all sorts of fresh grasses and related plants. You can get an idea of how important this type of food is for rabbits by the fact that wild rabbits feed primarily on green food items and do not take any grains. Green food is very nutritious and rich in vitamins and minerals. At certain times of the year

Your rabbit will enjoy vegetables from your own garden. They must be thoroughly washed before being fed to the rabbit.

(especially during summer months) it can even be used as a substitute for dietary concentrates (protein foods).

Because of the available variety of fruit and vegetables, we are now essentially independent of seasonal foods. Yet, during spring and summer we can still enrich our rabbit's diet with a few self-collected supplements. A number

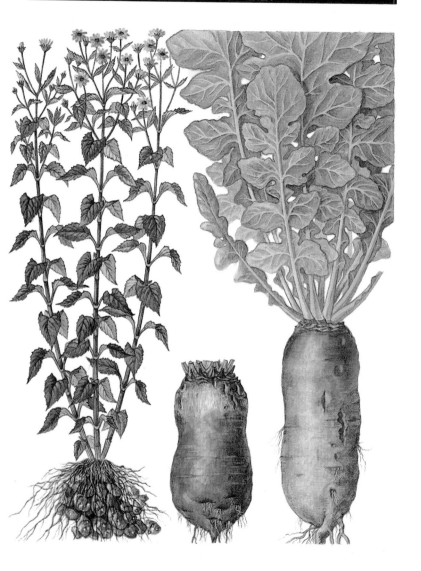

of foods can be planted in our garden, and some choice tidbits (parsley!) can even be cultivated in pots kept on a balcony. But remember, while variety is a definite advantage, not every animal has the same preferences!

If you collect the green food yourself, you must know the most important plants involved. All rabbits favor dandelion. Other eagerly eaten foods include grasses, shepherd's purse, sorrel, chickweed, groundsel, bindweed, wild radish, young nettle, yellow clover, and others.

Opposite: Many plants that produce tubers edible by humans can also be fed to rabbits.

Unless you are familiar with native plants, a suitable handbook to identify different species is often very helpful, especially one that tells you how to stay away from those plants that are poisonous for rabbits. These include: belladonna, meadow saffron, hemlock, marsh mallow, nightshade (solanum), dogbane, darnell grass, and others.

Quite suitable and also eagerly eaten by rabbits are the leaves of carrot, radish and turnip. Then there are carrots (as such), endive, chicory, swedes, turnips, celery, field lettuce, spinach, apple, pear, Chinese cabbage, corn (on the cob) and parsley. Some green foods must be used with caution since they will cause severe flatulence in most rabbits. These include potatoes, head lettuce and all types of cabbage. It is better to do without them! Germinating potatoes and beans are poisonous to rabbits, and so these products must never be fed.

Although most essential minerals are included in a well-balanced diet of basic foods, including green food, most rabbits do like to use a calcium or salt licking stone, also known as a salt spool.

DRINKING WATER

The need for water among rabbits can vary substantially from one animal to the next. Once,

A rabbit grown for meat purposes.

Marsh marigold, or cowslip (left), buttercup (center), and
larkspur. All of these decorative plants are poisonous to rabbits.

I kept two male rabbits for a while under identical climatic conditions. One of these animals drank nearly 500 ml water per day, while the other one appeared to be quite satisfied with the moisture in its green food and did not drink at all. Consequently, we will have to experiment with how much drinking water each particular animal needs. Normally, every rabbit should have constant access to water, even if it gets an ample supply of green food. If both are given simultaneously, than you can even do without the vitamin preparations, which are commercially available as supplements to drinking water.

Fresh clean water should be available to your pet at all times.

Make sure that the nozzle of the water bottle is not located directly above the food bowl or bedding hay. These devices have a tendency to release occasional drops of water that can spoil grain food or hay.

Opposite: A gravity-fed water bottle prevents a rabbit from soiling its water.

A Siamese smoke pearl Netherland Dwarf.

Living With a Rabbit

Once you arrive home with your new pet there is a great temptation to immediately pick it up and put it on your lap and generously stroke and caress it. You would not be doing the scared little animal a favor! Just think what your pet has just gone through! It has just been torn away from its accustomed surroundings

and its siblings and stuffed into a more or less dark box. It then was probably severely shaken during the transport, only to re-emerge to daylight and totally new surroundings and a multitude of new impressions. Of course, the poor animal is scared and will flinch every time it is touched or hears unfamiliar noises.

Therefore, it is best to put the rabbit into its cage for the time being, so that it can adjust to the new sights, sounds and odors. It depends on the individual animal as

Opposite: Ideally, the ears of a Netherland Dwarf should be two inches in length.

to how long this process of adjustment takes. Scared rabbits (especially those that have already had traumatic experiences in the past) may need weeks, while more sedate animals may have adjusted in only two or three days.

During the period of adjustment, you not only have to do without handling and petting the rabbit, but initially you must also not attempt to feed the rabbit by hand. You can do this once the animal has calmed down. This is easily recognizable, for instance, when it no longer sits in one corner of the cage with its eyes dilated and when it continues to breathe normally even though it may hear an uncommon

noise. An unmistakable sign that the animal has settled in is when the animal rolls over on its side and remains in that position totally relaxed. It will only do that when it feels completely at ease in its surroundings. One way to tame the rabbit— or other animals for that matter—is by offering tasty tidbits. Hold a carrot or a piece of apple, or— better yet—a dandelion leaf into the cage. Do not follow the animal if it flees, because this would set the animal under renewed stress. Sooner or later the rabbit will submit to the tempting odor of the

Opposite: Beware of poison hemlock (left), jimsonweed (center), and water hemlock—all are poisonous.

food and come over to your hand. The fear arising from the unaccustomed odor of your hand will soon be overcome by appetite, and the rabbit will take the food. It will attempt, of course, to pull the food out of your hand, so hold on to it gently. It can happen that the animal will then let go and withdraw. But do not worry, it will try again and again until it eventually starts to feed. This completes the first step in the animal's training program. Once the animal has been taking food from your hand for several days, you can attempt the second step. Reach around with the other hand and gently touch the animal, preferably on the forehead. The

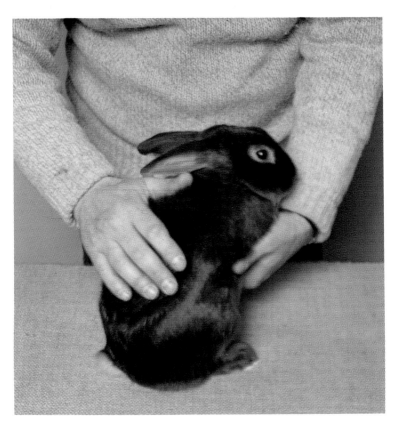

Do not overhandle your rabbit when you first bring him home. If he responds to your touch in a nervous fashion, let him alone.

animal is used to being touched at that spot (roughly between the eyes) by its siblings; it is sort of a rabbit 'greeting.' If the animal does not object, then move your finger up the forehead to a spot between the ears and there gently scratch the animal. Do not be surprised if the animal suddenly pulls its head back: it may just not be quite ready yet for such intimacies. Try it again next time! The largest hurdle has been overcome once the rabbit lets you touch its head. From then on you can gradually work your hand over the entire body of the animal. You must, however, remember that some rabbits are ticklish along their belly, and touching them there is often resented. In general, a rabbit normally does not inflict a severe bite, but even the most peaceful animal can nip or scratch. Talking to the animal in a calm voice often facilitates the taming process; it calms the animal down and makes it familiar with your voice. Soon your pet will come to the front of the cage when you approach, and it may even let you pet it without being bribed with a tasty morsel. From then on it is only a small step until the animal thrusts itself towards your hand in order to be stroked and caressed.

Keep repeating its name when stroking the animal. It learns to associate this with something pleasant and it will react accordingly. But, please, do not be too disappointed if all this does not work with your pet rabbit. Even among animals can we find smart ones and those that are less intelligent, those that are keen to learn and those that are just plain lazy!

Only after your rabbit is completely hand-tame should it be permitted to run freely outside its cage. Trying to capture a rabbit that is not completely tame can turn into a wild chase, which is neither good for the health of the animal nor its trust in humans.

This could destroy your relationship with your pet before it even had a chance to develop properly.

CORRECT HANDLING

Picking up a rabbit correctly must be learned, otherwise you may injure or hurt the animal. The long ears were not intended as 'handles.' You must *never* pick up a rabbit by its ears. It would kick its legs in panic and so endanger its own neck. A rabbit treated—or rather mistreated—in this fashion will lose all trust in its keeper. Children and hesitant adults tend to pick up a rabbit just like they would a cat, by reaching with both hands around its abdomen in order to pick up the animal. There is nothing wrong with this in practice, but immediately after being lifted up the animal's legs must find some support. If this is not found quickly, the

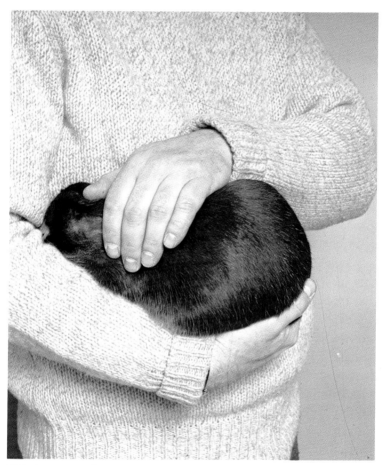

This is an excellent way to carry your rabbit around. It helps the animal to feel safe and secure.

abdominal organs are being squeezed. In other words, this grip is suitable for lifting but not for carrying. Most rabbits will kick if picked up in this manner, either out of fear or because they are ticklish in that region. Their strong claws can inflict deep cuts, and the sudden pain may cause you to drop the animal, which can cause injury to him.

The safest and least dangerous grip is that onto the shoulder pelt—even though it may be difficult for a sensitive person since it looks a bit like hanging the animal. It is imperative that you reach for the shoulder pelt and not the neck pelt, otherwise you would strangle your pet! Young rabbits must not be picked up in this manner, because their skin is still too delicate for such strain. The advantage of this method is that the rabbit does not struggle (except if your grip is not firm enough or if it is afraid that it might fall). Pick up the animal in the following manner: with one hand, grip the shoulder pelt, and with your other hand, reach under the hindlegs in order to support it.

If you want to carry the animal for a while, place it on your lower arm, which is angled against your body (similar to carrying a human baby), and support the shoulder region with your free hand, so that it cannot slip down.

THE CONTENTED RABBIT

The two most favorite occupations of your rabbit are feeding and running. Wild rabbits spend most of their lives on the move, in search of food or to flee from a threat. A domesticated rabbit does not have to search for food, so your pet must be offered 'occupational' food. Similarly, a pet rabbit does not have to flee from an enemy, but it must be able to release its running urge. A rabbit that is never let out of its cage becomes apathetic and can get fat. In principle, this has nothing to do with being locked up (that is, imprisonment in human terms) but simply with the fact that some rabbit cages are too small to permit the animal a good 'run.' In an appropriately sized cage, there is sufficient room for an average-sized rabbit (and in particular for a dwarf rabbit), so that it can be left in there—in good conscience—for a few days without being let out for a run. However, if your pet has to live in a standard cage, it should be given at least an hour's exercise every day. All you have to do is let it out, and it will look after its own exercise needs. For some this may only be a leisurely stroll from the cage over to its favorite resting spot somewhere in the room. But on the next day, the animal may be racing through the room doing somersaults. 'Being chased' is only fun if it is your pet's idea. If the

animal keeps running towards you and then dashes away again, leaping into the air and shaking its head, then it is in a playful mood and wants to be played with.

Most rabbits are not interested in toys. One of my animals totally ignored balls but was intrigued by a scrunched-up paper ball. This paper ball was chewed on, picked up with the teeth and tossed about. Rabbits play in similar fashion with small twigs. They are curious animals and like to investigate caves and other hiding places. They can keep themselves busy for hours with a large carton with a number of access holes, and they like to disappear behind furniture.

DANGERS OUTSIDE THE CAGE

Here we have to distinguish between the rabbit being in danger and the rabbit endangering the surroundings. Rabbits like to gnaw, and they are not fussy about what they select—wall paper, furniture, carpets, even electrical cables! It should be noted here, though, that there are 'dedicated chewers,' as well as those animals that do not chew or gnaw at all. Offering your rabbit 'chewing foods' in the form of dried bread, branches or

Opposite: No matter how small your rabbit is, its hindquarters should always be supported when the animal is lifted.

crackers increases the probability that he will leave your furniture alone. It is obvious that chewing on an electrical cable can have fatal consequences for your pet. Some rabbits show a distinct preference for indoor plants, which seems like an appropriate lead-in for a discussion on the dangers that can be lurking when a rabbit is let out of its cage. Here I must point out that many of our popular indoor plants are poisonous. Make sure that your pet cannot reach the plants. Very tame rabbits often try to follow their owner out of the room, or even wait at the door for his or her return. Therefore, you must exercise caution when opening or closing

doors and always keep an eye out as to where the animal is in the room. Always keep chemicals (e.g., household cleaners and detergents) and items like full ash trays out of reach of your pet rabbit. Domesticated rabbits often lack the survival instincts of wild rabbits to leave inedible substances alone; substances like that, within reach of your pet, can lead to fatal poisoning.

If your rabbit likes to jump up on the couch, please be careful where you sit down! Maybe your favorite spot is already occupied by your rabbit, resting comfortably among the pillows. If you also own a dog or cat or even a large parrot, and these

A Silver rabbit.

animals cannot get along with your long-eared pet, make sure the animals are kept apart in separate rooms (or that the parrot is kept in its cage). Always close the door behind you when you leave the room, even if it is only for a brief moment!

CAN A RABBIT BE TRAINED?

The answer is yes, to some extent. You can housetrain a rabbit and teach it to leave certain things alone. Most rabbits are determined to urinate in a particular location, preferably this is inside the cage, which should always be left open when the rabbit is roaming about in the room. Some animals, however, tend to find another 'toilet spot' once they are outside the cage, usually somewhere in a corner. Maybe they are attracted to that site by a particular odor or something else; nobody knows the real answer to why rabbits prefer particular sites. If you want to stop your rabbit from using your carpet as a 'urinal,' I suggest you put the cage, or simply a pan with cat litter, on that particular spot. If you do that, the rabbit usually also deposits its droppings in there. If, however, your long-eared pet drops its little pellets all over the room, you simply pick them up with a paper tissue or dust pan and then throw them onto the 'rabbit toilet.' If the animal is halfway smart, it can learn what is expected of it.

I have taught my rabbits that there are certain things and places that are 'off limits,' using a particular teaching technique. To get my point across to the animal, I select a

An assortment of young Netherland Dwarfs. All are under the age of five months.

strategically suitable place, where I sit down armed with a pocket (traveler's) pack of paper tissues. When the rabbit is trying to investigate (eyes wide open, ears pointing forward, body extended for its full length), say, the floor-length curtains, I emit a shrill whistle and throw the pack of paper tissues at the rear end of the animal. This pack is soft and light enough not to injure the animal, yet makes a sufficient impact to scare it off. Because of the distance effect, the rabbit would not associate this scare with me but rather with the whistle and the particular location where it was frightened off. In typical rabbit fashion the animal would then 'thump' the floor with both hind legs and turn away. If it comes over to me, it is lavishly petted. After about two weeks, the animal is fully whistle-conditioned. This method also works most of the time with other objects or locations. I am making a point by saying 'most of the time,' because sometimes temptation clearly overwhelmed the animal. For instance, one of my rabbits was always determined to disappear behind a particular piece of furniture. Since there were several electrical cables in that area, I was determined to keep the animal away from it. However, occasionally the animal would deliberately ignore that. Pretending to be totally disinterested, the rabbit would slowly head towards the 'off limits' area, then suddenly it would 'thump' and with a giant leap it would disappear behind that piece of furniture. This then, of course, required direct intervention by me. The interesting observation here is the 'warning thump,' which seems to express surmounting reluctance and guilty conscience by the animal. (By the way, gaps between adjacent pieces of furniture can be easily 'plugged up' with bottles of suitable sizes.)

PROVIDING COMPANY FOR YOUR RABBIT

If you cannot give enough time to your rabbit, you should consider getting a playmate for your pet. Any fear that this will cause your well-established pet to lose its tameness is totally unfounded. As I have mentioned, a guinea pig or chinchilla can be suitable company for your rabbit. Keep in mind that the established animal has 'home advantage' and defends its territory against any intruder. For that reason you must never put both animals simultaneously into the same cage together. Use separate cages and put them closely side by side, so that both animals can see and smell each other but cannot come into direct contact (to bite!). After the newly arrived animal has settled in, let it out into the room by itself, so that it can explore the new surroundings in peace. Repeat this for a few days and only then let the established animal out at the same time. Closely watch the rabbit! It can happen that there is some 'sparring,' but that is nothing to worry about. If the territorial owner starts to pursue the newcomer relentlessly, you should intervene and separate the animals. Do not make the mistake of confining the established animal to its cage while you leave the newcomer outside. Your pet would interpret this as being due to the newcomer and not its own behavior, and so at the next opportunity 'old' would attack 'new' even more vigorously.

You have to be particularly watchful when you put a guinea pig together with your pet rabbit. Guinea pigs rarely ever defend themselves and so they are vulnerable to quite a serious beating. On the other hand, a chinchilla is far more agile than even the fastest rabbit. It is also a far more powerful 'jumper,' and can—if need be—escape by jumping onto furniture.

Placing two rabbits together requires additional considerations. Two uncastrated bucks cannot be put together at all. Similarly, an uncastrated male will severely harass a castrated male, so that this sort of combination is also unworkable. This then leaves us with the possibilities of two females or two castrated males, unless you want to keep a pair and then

A rabbit enjoying the outdoors with his guinea pig pals.

continuously put up with their progeny and find suitable homes for them.

Male rabbits are also sexually inclined towards females of other species and therefore can really get on the nerves of such cagemates. For instance, I once kept a rabbit buck together with a female guinea pig. Although she was the 'boss' in the cage, the animal did suffer considerably from being hounded by the male rabbit when he was amorously inclined. Finally, I offered the female a small sleeping box inside the cage, where the much larger male rabbit could not follow. Others among my male rabbits have sexually pursued female chinchillas and—in one case—even a tame female rat! Consequently, caution must be exercised when putting a 'mixed' pair together.

KEEPING RABBITS AND OTHER PETS TOGETHER

Guinea pigs and chinchillas have already been mentioned as rabbit companions. What about other pets as companions for your rabbit? Both a dog and a cat must at first be closely supervised, so that their innate hunting instinct does not come to the surface; primarily young and very timid rabbits are endangered in such associations. Yet, a fully grown and assertive rabbit can indeed be an

Rabbits and guinea pigs can get along well. If you own one of each, feeding will be a simple matter because they both eat many of the same things.

equal partner with a larger animal; in fact, it can even become the dominant partner. I know of one case, for instance, where a large and powerful rabbit with a well-developed self-confidence very severely beat up a visiting, impressive-looking (but still very young) Rottweiler. The dog became so intimidated that for a long time thereafter he did not dare to go inside the house where he had been treated so badly!

Small rodents, such as striped squirrels, hamsters, mice and rats usually get along quite well with rabbits, but they are often ignored or unintentionally run over! Similarly, there are no problems either with small cage birds or tortoises. Large parrots (cockatoos, macaws, and related forms) can present problems if they become jealous of the rabbit. They can inflict serious injuries with their large and powerful beaks. Of course, an assertive rabbit will remember any rough treatment dished out by the bird, and there will be a 'pay back' at the next opportune time!

ESSENTIAL CARE

In regard to maintenance requirements, a rabbit is a pet that is easy to look after. This, however, does not mean that the essential care for such a pet can be largely ignored or even taken lightly. The cage must be cleaned once or twice a week. First, remove all bedding and newspapers. Then, the bottom tray must be thoroughly scrubbed and cleaned with a mild household detergent (do not use any substances with a strong odor!) or vinegar (effective against uric acid). Renew the bedding and newspaper, and also remember to replace soiled hay with fresh, new hay. Once a month the cage wire must also be washed off thoroughly.

Hot weather, together with high humidities, tends to expedite the decay of rabbit excrement; this in turn enhances the development of bacteria and fungi and also attracts flies. Therefore, during the peak of the summer, it is better to clean the cage more often than during the colder seasons, so as not to jeopardize the health of your long-eared pet. It may already be too late once the cage 'smells upwind!'

All watering equipment (bowls, bottles, etc.) should be rinsed out under hot water, before being refilled with fresh drinking water. Algae, which may have started to grow inside the glass bottles, can easily be removed with a bottle brush. All drinking water must be completely replaced every day.

Similarly, the food bowl will also have to be monitored closely for dried up food remnants and fecal pellets, or possibly even urine, which could have spoiled the food. The food bowl must be completely dry before it is filled up again with fresh food. Beyond that, it is self-explanatory that uneaten green food must be removed daily.

Rabbits take care of their fur by themselves, yet we can provide an additional grooming aid. Especially during the molting season, pet rabbits like to be brushed with a medium brush, which removes all dead hairs. The claws—just as human finger and toe nails—grow continuously and need regular attention.

You must never give your rabbit a bath! This can lead to a serious respiratory infection; most certainly your pet would suffer a severe fright. A bath is really not required since a rabbit is as clean as a cat. The increasingly popular angora rabbits require one more grooming aid: their fur has to be clipped regularly (three to four times a year). If this is not done, their long hair will become matted, which may lead to the development of a heat and moisture barrier. This can be fatal for the animal if its fur is not groomed properly. You can consult a rabbit club or an angora breeder for expert advice on how to shear an angora rabbit correctly. They will also show you how to groom the animal once a week with a coarse comb.

HOLIDAY HINTS

When you go on holidays locally, you might consider taking

your pet rabbit along. But if you leave your state or country, there may be specific customs and/or quarantine regulations that can make it difficult for your pet to travel with you. If this is the case, leave your pet in the care of relatives or friends or possibly a local boarding facility. The daily costs are reasonable, and your rabbit is getting professional care. Moreover, your pet would not particularly enjoy a trip into a hot climate (southern Europe, Mexico, etc.); and once it

Regular grooming will help to keep your rabbit's coat in tiptop condition.

has recovered from the trip, then the traumatic return journey starts. If the animal is traveling with you, make sure (well in advance) that pets are permitted wherever you intend to stay.

If you are traveling by car, make sure the cage is secured (and cannot slide) and protected against direct sun exposure. Put enough hay inside the cage that in the event you have to hit the brakes hard, the animal does not get thrown around. While traveling, the animal belongs in its cage and *not* on the laps of your children, in spite of their protests! Not only could the animal become a virtual missile when the car has to break very hard, but it could also jump down onto the front car floor and so become a serious danger among the foot pedals.

Food and drinking water containers should be removed for the journey. Arrange for a rest stop every three hours or so, and give your pet an opportunity to drink and feed. But remember that the journey could have frightened the animal so much that it may refuse all food!

By the way, for a three-week holiday it is not that critical if your rabbit does not get to run around outside its cage every day; the animal can do well without it for such a short period of time. Once the animal has returned home, the daily excursion outside the cage must then become a routine again.

AN OUNCE OF PREVENTION

Correct accommodation and proper feeding and care lessen the risk of diseases for your pet considerably. Here too, the motto is: prevention is better than healing. Even though it may not look like it sometimes, your pet does not get ill deliberately in order to spoil your planned weekend excursion. Instead, you may have made a mistake in your animal husbandry efforts! Therefore, it is important to watch for those early signs indicating a health problem. Should you notice anything unusual, take the animal to a veterinarian or at least consult an experienced rabbit breeder. The only first aid you can provide is for diarrhea and constipation.

Diarrhea: This can occur after the animal has been kept (temporarily) too cold, is exposed to a draft, or eats spoiled or the wrong kind of food (e.g., soiled bedding). The feces becomes soft to almost fluid-like and has a foul smell. Keep the animal at room temperature and out of any draft (and *off* the floor). Green food must NOT be given until the animal is clearly

better. Offer dried (pelletized) food, lots of hay and some boiled (well dried) rice, together with lukewarm camomile tea (instead of water).

Constipation: Finding your animal hunched up with an arched back and a bloated abdomen, refusing all food, is a typical symptom of constipation. Offer lots of water, as well as carrots and lettuce. Movement also contributes to the healing process.

Mucoid enteritis (enterotoxemia): This disease is often referred to as bloat or scours. It is caused by green food that was either wet, too cold or had started to ferment (kept too warm), or by those types of food that cause flatulence. The abdomen of the animal is bloated, in this case by the formation of gases inside the intestine. The animal also has respiratory problems and rolls from side to side since it has pressure pains. Remove all food immediately and take the animal to a veterinarian. This disease is often fatal, and so great haste in providing expert veterinary care is essential.

Other problems: You should also consult a veterinarian if you notice any of the following symptoms (do *not* attempt to treat these yourself): coughing, frequent sneezing, discharge from nose and ears, swellings, rapid weight loss, bare patches on the skin, cramp-like twitching and diarrhea in conjunction with flatulence (as opposed to mucoid enteritis, discussed above). The reasons for all these problems and symptoms are diverse, and it is often difficult for the beginner to make a correct diagnosis. Prepare yourself for the (sometimes substantial) veterinary charges, which can be much higher than what you originally paid for the animal! An animal is not a decorative object that you can throw away and replace with a new one! If this enters your mind when you have to decide on seeking veterinary care for your animal, you are *not* a responsible pet owner.

The Rabbit Family

Breeding rabbits—even if this means rearing only a single litter—requires certain decisions that should be made early. Nursing females must be left undisturbed, otherwise they abandon or even kill their young. Therefore, during that period, you and your children will have to do without your pet playmate! Young rabbits need a lot of room to run and exercise. That means that not only do you have to watch one animal running around in a room, but indeed several! More animals also means more cage space is required. Maybe you do not have a taker immediately for every animal. This then means you have to keep one or more animals all in sufficiently large cages. More animals also means more food is required. Also, there will be more cage cleaning and greater demands on the bedding, hay and straw supply! Only after you have decided that you are prepared to accept all this should you proceed with your plans to produce progeny from your pet rabbit.

MATING RABBITS

It is of fundamental importance to keep in mind when mating rabbits that the female (doe) must always be put into the cage with the male (buck), and NOT the other way around! Even a female rabbit in heat will always treat the male as an intruder into her territory and attack him relentlessly with teeth and claws. But in the unfamiliar surroundings of the male's cage, the female loses her assertiveness and accepts the male

Opposite: If you do not have the time and resources to devote to raising a rabbit family, you should not breed your rabbit.

normally without a fight. If you have only a single female to be mated, you can take it to a professional rabbit breeder or to a friend who owns a suitable buck. A female rabbit in heat can be recognized by the slightly swollen (reddish) vaginal region and her general restlessness (she scratches around a lot and attempts to build a nest).

A doe in heat is 'courted' by the buck. He will emit grumbling sounds and will hop around the female with his posterior region curiously lifted up. He may also 'mark' her with urine, a typical rabbit behavior used to delineate territories (i.e., "she is mine"). Finally, there is the actual mating, for which the female lays flat on her abdomen, with her posterior section raised up. The buck mounts the female from behind, biting into her neck fur, and copulation proceeds. Sometimes the female manages to slip away at the last moment and so prevents a successful mating. After a successful copulation, the buck slides off the doe sideways and remains next to her for a brief period, breathing heavily and exhausted. The animals can be separated again after the mating has been completed.

BIRTH AND REARING THE YOUNG

If the mating was successful, the doe will become restless again within a few days, scratching along the bottom of the cage and again attempting to build a nest. From then on, the pregnant doe needs a particularly well-balanced diet, as well as a lot of peace and quiet. Please do *not* pick up the animal (unless it cannot be avoided) and do *not* carry the cage around. Provide sufficient drinking water and offer lots of hay and straw, which the doe uses to build a nest.

You can also put a special nursery box inside the cage, where the doe can build her nest. She feels particularly safe and secure in there. (After all, domesticated rabbits originated from burrowing wild rabbits.)

The gestation period lasts from 28 to 31 days. The doe's abdominal region swells, more or less, depending upon the anticipated litter's size. About a week before giving birth, the female starts to pull fur from her abdominal region and begins to pad the nest, so that the young—born blind and naked—have a soft and warm nest. A sudden, slender appearance of the female is the sign that birth of the litter has taken place. During the first few days after having dropped the litter, the female is particularly sensitive to disturbances. One or two days after the birth, you should attempt to divert the female's attention—when she is away from the nest—by offering food or patting her; with the other hand you cautiously check the nest. Do not touch any of the young; only remove any dead ones or remnants of afterbirth. If all is well, you will see a nest full of pink, totally helpless beings, which will develop during the following weeks into a happy bunch of little bunnies. Litter sizes vary, depending upon the rabbit breed. Pure-bred dwarfs rarely produce more than four young, mixed miniature breeds up to eight young, and larger breeds sometimes up to twelve young.

In contrast to other small mammals, young rabbits do not get a number of small feedings of milk from their mother, but often only a single large feeding per day. Even though the open nest may be inviting, do *not* constantly poke around in it. Perform only a single inspection of the young per day! Constant harassment can cause the female to abandon her young! For three weeks the young will feed on nothing but milk from the doe; after that they start taking solid food. They are fully weaned after six weeks. That is the earliest point at which they can be separated from their mother, but it is best to leave them with their mother for another two weeks before the family is broken up.

ORPHANED YOUNG

Weakened from the trauma of giving birth or due to disease, it can happen that a nursing female dies, leaving

A mother rabbit nursing her young. The size of rabbit litters can vary among breeds.

behind a nest full of young. What can be done in a case like that? Fortunately, so far I have never had to face a problem like that, therefore I can only pass on the experiences of others. If the babies are less than a week old, there is really only a very slim chance to save them. Older animals can be raised with a bottle or a foster mother. Should you try the latter, you have to find a suitable (lactating) female, unless you happen to be so lucky as to have another nursing female. With such a prospective foster mother on hand, you have to cautiously prevent her from returning to her own nest for at least one-half hour. During that time you have to place the orphaned young into the nest of the foster mother, together with her young, in order to pick up the new nest odor. If the odor of the orphaned young is not the same as that of her own, she will not accept them; in fact, she may even kill them.

After half an hour or so, the female is permitted to return to her nest. If she remains calm and looks after the entire (enlarged) litter, your attempt appears to have succeeded; it is unlikely that there will be hostilities later on. If, on the other hand, the female seems uneasy, she should be closely watched for another hour or so, to find out whether she has detected the orphans and will attempt to harm them.

Rabbit females do not seem to know how many young their litter has; everything that has their nest odor will be accepted as their own progeny. Yet, the number of young per 'litter' cannot be increased indefinitely. If an intended foster female already has a large number of young, she is hardly capable of raising additional ones. Their best chances are with a doe that nurses only one or two young.

Should the intended foster female reject the orphaned young, you can make another attempt a few hours later. Should that one fail too, you have to consider raising the young on the bottle. There have been rare cases where young rabbits have been raised by nursing cats, but these have been very quiet and tolerant cats.

For hand rearing, you need a small nursing bottle, as is available from pet shops or toy stores. In an emergency, you can also use a small pipette. The young have to learn to suck properly from such a substitute 'mother,' and this may require some patience. A suitable feeding formula can be baby milk or unsweetened condensed milk, which is diluted 50/50 with water and supplemented with a multi-vitamin preparation. As the young get larger, you can also add thinned-out (cooked) oatmeal and carrot juice. In order to be safe, you may wish to consult a veterinarian or have him examine the young; he should be able to give you a few useful hints.

Experts are divided on how many meals per day the young should be given. Wild and domesticated rabbits usually nurse their young only once every 24 hours, so that a single daily feeding seems to be the most natural feeding regimen. Others suggest four to six feedings daily, each of correspondingly smaller volumes of milk formula. This, however, should really only be required for very weak, abandoned young.

Young rabbits need a lot of warmth. The implement for that purpose is a hot water bottle placed underneath the nest and re-filled at regular intervals. It is important, however, that the nest temperature not exceed 32 degrees C. Similarly, as with human babies, the milk given must be approximately body temperature. Each of the young should get a gentle 'tummy rub' after each feeding. This simulates the licking by the mother to enhance the digestion in the young. Without this 'massage,' the young can develop digestive difficulties, which can have fatal consequences! If you are successful in hand-rearing the young, you will end up with particularly tame pet rabbits! Inevitably, it is then very difficult to part from these 'bottle children' once they have become adult rabbits.

FINDING GOOD HOMES FOR THE RABBITS

Now, what to do with all these rabbits? Ideally you should have lined up prospective homes already before the young were born, preferably even before the parents were mated. Ask around among relatives, friends, or pet shops, whether anybody is interested in

Opposite: A female rabbit with her babies in a box designed specifically for nesting purposes.

taking some of the animals. If there is a rabbit fanciers' or breeders' club, check with them if they want the young rabbits, especially if the male came originally from them. If your female is a genuine dwarf, you may wish to show her to the local pet shop owner. Genuine dwarfs are easier to sell, and so he may be more interested. If you advertise the animals, you should do this early, that is, when the young reach the age of four weeks or so, and let prospective customers select a particular animal from the litter. They can then pick it up about four weeks later. This protects the animals from spontaneous buyers, who may quickly lose interest again in their new pet.

Animal lovers who are prepared to wait four weeks for their new pet are—as a rule—more genuinely interested and will come back to pick up the animal. This enhances the possibility that your rabbits will get into good hands.

A final tip: do not advertise your animals as being free-of-charge, unless you are not really interested in their welfare. It can happen that a reptile keeper will knock on your door in search of food for his giant snakes! Although snakes are very interesting animals and they too must live, this should hardly be the fate of your pet rabbits! Insist on selling the rabbits; a true animal lover does not haggle for a bargain!

When a female rabbit becomes pregnant, you will be able to see her grow noticeably larger.

Suggested Reading

All About Rabbits
  by Howard Hirschhorn
  ISBN 0-87666-760-4
  TFH M-543
  Hard cover, 5 1/2 x 8",
  96 pages, 32 full-color
  photos, 39 black and
  white photos

Lop Rabbits
  by Sandy Crook
  ISBN 0-86622-137-9
  TFH PS-809
  Hard cover, 5 1/2 x 8",
  192 pages, 100 full-color
  photos

**Encyclopedia of Pet
  Rabbits**
  by D. Robinson
  ISBN 0-87666-911-9
  TFH H-984
  Hard cover, 5 1/2 x 8",
  320 pages, 231 full-color
  photos, 52 black and
  white photos

Rabbits as a Hobby
  by Bob Bennett
  ISBN 0-86622-417-3
  TFH TT-003
  Soft cover, 7 x 10", 96
  pages, 118 full-color
  photos

Dwarf Rabbits
  by Günther Flauaus
  ISBN 0-86622-671-0
  TFH H-1073
  Hard cover, 5 1/2 x 8",
  128 pages, 73 full-color
  photos

Index

TW-121

The Proper Care of
Dwarf Rabbits

Michael Mettler